BERNIE MADOFF AND THE CRISIS

BERNIE MADOFF AND THE CRISIS

THE PUBLIC TRIAL OF CAPITALISM

COLLEEN P. EREN

STANFORD BUSINESS BOOKS

An Imprint of Stanford University Press • Stanford, California

Stanford University Press
Stanford, California

Printed in the United States of America on acid-free, archival-quality paper

Library of Congress Cataloging-in-Publication Data

Names: Eren, Colleen P., author.

Title: Bernie Madoff and the crisis : the public trial of capitalism /
  Colleen P. Eren.

Description: Stanford, California : Stanford University Press, 2017. |
  Includes bibliographical references and index.

Identifiers: LCCN 2016055521 (print) | LCCN 2016057613 (ebook) | ISBN
  9780804795586 (cloth : alk. paper) | ISBN 9781503602724 (pbk. : alk.
  paper) | ISBN 9781503603066 (electronic)

Subjects: LCSH: Madoff, Bernard L.—In mass media. | Global Financial Crisis,
  2008–2009—Press coverage—United States. | Global Financial Crisis,
  2008–2009—Press coverage—Great Britain. | Capitalism—Press
  coverage—United States. | Capitalism—Press coverage—Great Britain. |
  Commercial crimes—Press coverage—United States. | Commercial
  crimes—Press coverage—Great Britain.

Classification: LCC HV6692.M33 E74 2017 (print) | LCC HV6692.M33 (ebook) |
  DDC 364.16/8092—dc23

LC record available at https://lccn.loc.gov/2016055521

Typeset by Classic Typography in 11/15 Minion Pro

CONTENTS

ACKNOWLEDGMENTS

The loneliness of the long-distance runner is perhaps only matched by the loneliness of the first-time author. I am grateful to all those who joined me in some capacity on the journey.

Deep thanks go to my mentor and friend, Lynn Chancer. She has helped cultivate this project through many long and lovely conversations over coffee in Park Slope, and has been an unwavering source of support and belief in me. Thanks also to Michael Jacobson from the CUNY Institute of State and Local Governance, for offering his thoughts and critiques on an early rendition. I am saddened that Jock Young passed before the publication of this book, but am honored he was able to make his imprint on it, and grateful for his liberating insistence that I should "have some fun with it."

Criminologist Michael Levi's extensive work on white-collar crime and media has helped inspire and inform my own. I am grateful he was able to offer his comments and invaluable suggestions as a peer reviewer for this work. Many thanks also are due to my anonymous reviewer for her recommendations, particularly for changes to the first and last chapters.

I am truly appreciative to each of my interviewees, including John Nester of the Securities and Exchange Commission, Bernie Madoff, playwright Deb Margolin, and the dozens of UK and US journalists, editors, and photographers from *Barron's*, the *Daily Mail*, *Daily Mirror*, *Daily News*, *Financial Times*, *Guardian*, *Independent*, *New York Times*, *New York Post*, London *Times*, and *Washington Post*. In spite of often being on deadline, they shared their thoughts and experiences with me and strongly encouraged me to pursue this work. They have convinced me that journalists are at heart sociologists—but with better time-management skills. This book would not have been possible without their participation. Special thanks to Diana Henriques of the *New York Times* who shared willingly of her knowledge, reflections, and passion for the topic.

Deep gratitude to the editorial staff at Stanford University Press, particularly my marvelous editor, Margo Beth Fleming, for her enthusiasm, confidence, vision, and guidance through an unfamiliar process.

Thanks too to my colleagues at the City University of New York, especially to Dave Hill for his generous comments and suggestions during the revision process. And to Camila Gelpi-Acosta, John Chaney, Cory Feldman, Jill Kehoe, and Jennifer Wynn for their friendship and for fighting the good fight in bringing a critical criminological perspective to our students.

Endless appreciation is owed to my mother, Patricia Duggan Eren. Anything I will ever accomplish academically or otherwise can trace its origin to time spent reading *The Adventures of Stanley Cane* and *Henry's Awful Mistake* together. To my sister Meg, equally willing to perform *Much Ado about Nothing* or jump out of a plane with me through the years. It breaks my heart that my father, Mehmet Eren, will not share in this moment. But his influence, and that of my grandparents Larry and Ronny, on my life transcends all boundaries.

And to Elias Hernandez. You really are always that wonderful, and this book is for you.

BERNIE MADOFF AND THE CRISIS

on the same theme, Snider notes, "Many of the most serious antisocial and predatory acts committed in modern industrial countries are corporate crimes . . . Corporate crime costs far more than street crimes." She is concerned, like Reiman, with the power of ideology and, for instance, takes on the critical issue of regulation. Her article "The Sociology of Corporate Crime: An Obituary"[34] argues that corporate crime *itself* can "disappear" (e.g., be defined out of existence) through the intervention of powerful groups and business elites, through their neoliberal claims that masquerade as truth. "The reception of these [neoliberal] claims . . . can only be understood by relating it to the hegemonic dominance of those interests who stood to benefit from their acceptance as 'truth.'" Without invoking the same type of Marxist language or mentioning capitalist ideology, Henry Pontell has pointed out how "fraud minimalists," when focusing on the causes of economic crisis, have avoided terms like "crime" or "fraud," and have downplayed that role in major financial debacles like the savings and loan scandal or the corporate and accounting scandals of the early 2000s. Public policy that attempts to prevent or control these instances from occurring in the future while ignoring the "white washing [of] white collar crime" are therefore doomed to fail.[35] Indeed, Neil Fligstein and Alexander Roerhkasse, when looking at the causes of fraud in the financial crisis of 2007–9, argue that fraud was widespread and that "the structure of firms and markets caused fraud"; "market breakdowns tend to be understood in terms of myopia and misrecognition rather than strategic or malevolent abuse."[36]

Bernie Madoff and the Crisis's focus on social reaction to the Madoff case, however, does not deal abstractly with social reactions; its deepest theoretical grounding is in literature that has analyzed actual media coverage of crimes. Scholarship focusing on how coverage produces meaningful cultural dialogues that expose attitudes, beliefs, and configurations of power during specific sociohistorical periods is especially significant. For those who have written with this orientation, news coverage is not seen solely as a reflection of hegemonic corporate power over media outlets which in turn present biased reportage.[37] Nor do they present the coverage as a form of social control.[38] Rather,

2 OUT OF THE BUSINESS SECTION, INTO THE FRONT PAGES

> I think it was instantly recognized that this is a global story and a big story. Not just a New York story. Not just a Wall Street story. Not just a business story, but the *top* story that was going to have a lot of legs.
>
> —Tomoeh Murakami Tse, *Washington Post*, personal interview

TIME MAGAZINE IN FEBRUARY 2009 released an ignominious list, the "25 People to Blame for the Financial Crisis."[1] Alongside former Countrywide Financial CEO Angelo Mozilo, who perfected the art of predatory lending, and the "Gorilla of Wall Street," Dick Fuld, CEO of the now bankrupt investment bank Lehman Brothers, was Bernie Madoff. But the rationale for Madoff's inclusion on this list, other than the overlap in time between his Ponzi and the financial crisis, was weak. For all of the harm caused by the Ponzi, he was not involved with the subprime fiasco. He did not engage in predatory lending, was not involved in the creation of collateralized debt obligations. He neither determined nor influenced the Federal Reserve's "easy money" policy which led to wild leveraging in the financial services industries and to a housing bubble. And certainly he was not cited by the Financial Crisis Inquiry Commission when they released their almost six-hundred-page report on the causes of the crisis. And yet as the *Time* article and many others implied, he became conflated with and inextricably linked to the crisis of 2008 and the subsequent hardships spawned by the worldwide recession. His case became a household topic of discussion—one that infuriated, moved, and provoked audiences. This dual process of conflation with the crisis and engagement with mass audiences transformed

Madoff from a mere con artist into the "Madoff Scandal," a larger-than-life arena in which issues central to the crisis (and far beyond the scope of his own Ponzi) could be discussed and contested.

How and why the case was able to perform this role, exiting the business pages to which financial affairs are typically consigned, becomes clear when we look at the recurring themes and frames in the media coverage of Madoff, but also through the narratives told about his case and its reportage by those most closely involved with its production: the journalists and editors themselves. In this chapter, I present my discussions with these news makers as though the journalists were in conversation with each other, because this most clearly highlights their common perspectives and helps the reader to see points of convergence and divergence. However, it should be noted that my interviews were conducted individually and at separate locations. The shared themes, narratives, and frames that emerged from these interviews are important as they are revelatory, not only about the Madoff case but also how they help explain the collective, public transformation of the story into an archetypal saga with implications for social institutions.

Those who study journalism from a social scientific perspective, notably the anthropologists S. Elizabeth Bird and Robert Dardenne, have theorized on the connection between the universal, human need for stories and modern news reportage. They note, "News plays a cultural role to that of myth by using familiar, recurring narrative patterns that help explain why it seems simultaneously novel, yet soothingly predictable."[2] Unlike those who would idealistically suggest that news is an objective, value-free documentation and conveyance of facts, Bird and Dardenne contend that the storytelling component of news means that it will necessarily go beyond this function. News *stories* don't merely tell; they aim for meaning and coherence among "a cultural lexicon of understandable themes." Bird and Dardenne aptly describe this process as cultural *work* performed by journalists, knowingly or unknowingly fitting a chronological series of facts and "characters" into already extant frameworks of reference which have a comforting narrative familiarity for the audience. An unintended consequence of this process, however, is that adhering to myths and stories that resonate in the reportage of "moral disorder news" upholds the status quo.[3] Thus, as Glasser and Ettema note, "The press not only legitimates the prevailing moral order but undermines its rationality by preempting critical attention to it."[4]

Among the mythological frames which made the Madoff case resonant, five stand out from my content analysis. First, the scam involved a (purportedly) single criminal engaged in a comparatively simple scheme, which plays into British and American individualistic cultural impulses. This also facilitated the conflation of Madoff with the crisis as it allowed those without extensive financial knowledge or sophistication to comprehend a white-collar offense that was transpiring at the same time as a major economic upheaval. Second, surrounding the crime was a family drama of epic proportions, analogous to those found in well-known Western canonical masterworks such as those of Shakespeare. Complementing this family narrative was the involvement of a tale-worthy sum of money—tens of billions of dollars. During a time when vast fortunes were being lost in an almost quotidian manner, the figure was still large enough to shock readers and viewers. A Ponzi involving "only" hundreds of thousands or even millions of dollars simply could not have the same ability to capture our imagination, or inspire bewilderment, wonder, anger, and intrigue. Additionally, the case counted among its victims well-known figures and celebrities in America and Britain, figures who had obtained a status that lent them an existence outside the realm of the ordinary. The case, furthermore, was not confined to the rich; it also affected more "sympathetic," ordinary people, and thereby invited narratives implying that the rich had taken advantage of the poor. Last, there was an ethnoreligious dimension to Madoff's affinity scheme that disproportionately affected those in the Jewish community. At one level, this aroused a strong sense of sympathy as many of the victims of the Ponzi occupied a historically persecuted minority group. For example, Holocaust survivor and memoirist Elie Wiesel was one of Madoff's most revered marks. At the same time, though, anti-Semitic thought has a long history within Western culture and, lamentably, some commentators and consumers placed

Madoff in a supposed continuum of mythical Jewish "betrayers" includ-ing Judas Iscariot and Shakespeare's Shylock. To make matters worse, this negative stereotyping occurred during a time in which blatant anti-Semitism was showing other signs of resurfacing. Together these nar-rative elements were interspersed throughout the coverage, providing a familiar repertoire that not only enabled the transmission of knowledge, but also ensured that Madoff could become a cultural touchstone for the discussion of larger issues.

Individualism, Madoff, and the Crisis Jumble

Remarkably few individuals were prosecuted for the mortgage and fi-nancial crisis of 2007–9. Indeed, the *New York Times* reported on the single case of a Wall Street executive to go to jail for crisis-related illegal-ity: Kareem Serageldin of Credit Suisse was sentenced in 2013 to thirty months for conspiring to hide $100 million in losses within the com-pany's mortgage-backed securities portfolio.[5] Such a lack of prosecution is a departure from that seen during the savings and loan scandals of the 1980s, when 1,098 defendants were charged (even though this was a frac-tion of those suspected of major thrift crime, and only 451 of them were sentenced to prison, with light median sentences of less than two years).[6] Ironically, some of the same factors which have led the U.S. Department of Justice to focus less on taking powerful Wall Street players to court are the ones that enabled the Madoff story to become an ideal vehicle for conversations about wrongdoing: the simplicity of his fraud and its involvement of a single transgressor.

Since the 1980s, the Justice Department has sought to extricate itself from complex, time-consuming cases that "would [be] infernally diffi-cult to explain to juries."[7] It also hasn't brought criminal charges against the leadership of large corporations and financial institutions, choos-ing to mete out deferred prosecution agreements and impose civil fines. Such was the case in 2012 when HSBC was fined $1.9 billion for its in-volvement in laundering hundreds of millions of dollars in Latin Amer-ican drug cartel money and terrorist financing, in addition to trading with OFAC-sanctioned countries. Yet individual cases of insider trading unrelated to the financial crisis, like that of Galleon Group hedge fund manager Raj Rajaratnam, continue to be criminally prosecuted—because they are less abstruse but also because targeting these offenders does not significantly undermine the continued unfettered functioning of the financial system, even though that system has needed to be resuscitated with billions in taxpayer bailouts when that same unfettering has proved catastrophic.

In the same way that the Justice Department has homed in on simple cases, the public was able to focus on a readily understandable white-collar case about a single offender via Madoff, rendering him a proxy for the wrongdoing inherent in the financial crisis. Those writing the story in the media for both broadsheet and tabloid newspapers, with the dramatic backdrop of potential economic collapse, frequently invoked "Madoff" and "The Crisis" in the same article, such that wittingly or unwittingly the two became synonymous. In the course of my conversations with the British and American journalists and editors, many of them noted the process of conflation that occurred. Some, like Alex Berenson at the *New York Times*, remarked that this responsibility partially lay with the readership, which was not able to separate the two:

> Madoff became conflated with the banks, with the anger at the banks. And so, [to] people who weren't financially sophisticated, it all became jumbled together . . . And that was another reason why the coverage was so, so intense.

Stephen Foley of the British *Independent* described a more active role for journalists in fostering this perception:

> I can understand why people do it [conflate the credit crisis with Madoff] . . . I mean, one of the great means of writing about the credit crisis is that Wall Street created a whole Ponzi scheme . . . The credit bubble was some sort of pyramid scheme, some sort of fraud on the American people. So if you believe that, then it's very easy to wrap those two together. Obviously I don't believe that about the credit crisis; I've never written it and I've argued against it constantly; but if you do . . . then it's obviously great fun to wrap Madoff together with scamps like [Lloyd] Blankfein and Jamie Dimon.

Washington Post correspondents Tomoeh Murakami Tse and Zachary Goldfarb, in separate interviews, echoed Berenson's and Foley's thoughts on the connection between public anger at the banks and Madoff, but added to it the dimension of a lack of identifiable wrongdoers in the larger scandal, and thus the public's displaced anger which sought a target. Murakami Tse indicated:

> I think [the Madoff case] came at a time when the public was looking for someone to blame, like a face of Wall Street. There was so much outrage, rightfully so, and I think everyone reacted viscerally to that. Because it happened during the financial crisis, the public reaction was magnified and therefore our response was magnified.

Goldfarb concurred:

> [The Madoff case] came out, of course, in December of '08 and that was some three or four months after the financial crisis was underway, and the financial crisis—while it yielded a lot of unsavory executives and banks— . . . I don't think really ever produced a person in handcuffs who you could blame and see go to jail, . . . if not for the illegal wrongdoing, then the practices of Wall Street. So even though what Bernie Madoff did wasn't directly tied in a way to the wrongdoing on Wall Street or the bad actions of Wall Street . . . I thought he offered at least publically, a mechanism to direct their anger at.

While Murakami Tse and Goldfarb do not say, as Berenson does, that everything became "jumbled" for a financially illiterate public, their responses suggest that such an agglomerative effect was inevitable because of the historic moment in which the Madoff case was situated and the psychosocial dynamic of the time, during which the need to punish was widely felt but no prosecutions were forthcoming. Andrew Clark, deputy business editor for the London *Times*, similarly reflected on the public anger seeking an object, but he wasn't concerned about the level of direct accountability for the fallout from the crisis:

> I think the public was very, very angry with the financial services industry. And they wanted villains, and here was an arguable villain bound tight, served up on a plate . . . I think in some ways the most interesting aspect of the whole is, did this guy get a particularly harsh rap because he became a poster boy for

the financial crisis? I wouldn't go as far as saying he was a scapegoat [but] . . . I think he certainly could easily be in a federal penitentiary that could be entirely populated by financiers of his lot.

Many of the reporters like Clark balked at the term "scapegoat" or qualified their usage of the term because of its exculpatory implications. One of the few who did not shy away from the label was Tom Leonard, at the time a Wall Street correspondent for the *Daily Telegraph*, who wrote that—through Madoff—the public found release: "Finally they got a Wall Street bogeyman":

I mean he became almost a scapegoat for it, the all-star scapegoat . . . He bore the weight of that. I think he didn't bear responsibility for the financial crisis of course, but he became symbolic of a certain type of shark on Wall Street who had played fast and loose with the money of ordinary people.

Binyamin Appelbaum of the *Washington Post* agreed that Madoff was perhaps erroneously conflated with the crisis, and added a tantalizing metaphor:

Madoff was in many ways a product of the era, but at the same time he wasn't a participant in its core themes, and I think . . . it's ironic and actually deeply troubling that what we've got out of the financial crisis was a series of convictions of people and . . . the sort of stapling of their heads on the pole along the bridge . . . You know, in England in the sixteenth century the heads that would be on Tower Bridge would be the wrong heads.

Whether the journalists chose to employ the terms "scapegoat" or "symbol" or "face of Wall Street" or "mechanism at which to direct anger," it is clear from these discussions that in addition to the temporal synchronicity of the Madoff case and the financial crisis, in their view a single-offender focus was also essential to the case's narrative appeal and consequent popularity. Some-*one* could now be held accountable—not an anonymous corporate entity, not abstruse financial instruments or abstract economic forces, but instead an actual culpable person. This individualizing process in the media and public discourse played directly into the propensity for cultural individualism in the United States and Britain, thus giving it frames that appealed to deep-seated emotions and sensibilities.[8] During the course of our interview in the *Guardian*'s offices in Soho, journalist Ed Pilkington reflected:

> You wonder why the Brits are so into it . . . It was based on one person, where Enron was very much a city story because it was a bad institution about [the] financial sort of skullduggery that your general public would find difficult to comprehend. This was about one man, persuading people to give him money. It was very simple, and very human. So everyone was interested.

Financial Times journalist David Gelles, who wrote about his jail-house interview with Madoff for the weekend magazine, likewise emphasized:

> This was the financial crisis writ large on a very personal level. This wasn't one of the financial institutions getting itself into another mess. This was an individual actor who had stolen billions of dollars from other individual actors and, of course, some smaller investment funds. But what I think was so amazing was that it personalized the financial crisis in a way that it's hard to do when so many of the previous stories had been so abstract.

For all of the attention on this Ponzi, focused as it was on an individual, conjecture as to external factors or influences that might have influenced his behavior did not emerge in my analysis as central to the reportage. But internal, psychological defects or idiosyncrasies were proposed to provide if not an explanation of the Ponzi then an indication of underlying pathologies as well as colorful anecdotes to stimulate the readership. The London *Times* reported on the eccentricities of Madoff's behavior as described by his secretary—his egomania, sexism, and even his penchant for massage parlors.[9] The *Times* also, in "More on the Bizarre World of Bernie,"[10] made note of his "psychological aberrations" as evinced through his fanaticism about the use of color schemes in his office—all grays and blacks. "For a man who liked everything square, working in an elliptical building in New York was therefore completely extraordinary. Bernie is the most anally retentive man I've ever met," Madoff's London office manager, Julia Fenwick, remarked for the *Daily Mail*.[11] The *New York Times*'s "The Talented Mr. Madoff" went further in presenting these characteristics—his "reclusiveness" and "aloofness," his obsessive-compulsive behaviors[12]—as indicative of some kind of serious underlying psychological problem, citing extensively J. Reid Meloy, a forensic psychologist who found similarities between Madoff and serial killer Ted Bundy.

Of course, tabloids like the *New York Post* and the *Daily News* had wider latitude to describe Madoff's criminogenic personality in more colorful headlines, but the content of their probes into his quirks and qualities did not differ substantially from that of the broadsheet/ elite papers. The *Post* labeled him a "Brazen Bum" and "Rat," declaring "Madoff, a Monster from Birth." Mary Jo Buttafuocco, survivor of a highly publicized homicide attempt in New York in the 1990s, was quoted in her assessment of Madoff as a classic sociopath.[13] The *Daily News* termed him "Ponz Scum,"[14] and the UK's *Daily Mirror*, a "slippery Wall Street wheeler-dealer."[15] Madoff as an individual, then—his obsessive-compulsive traits, his aloofness, his ability to con victims out of their lifesavings with an almost ruthless detachment—became the subject of analysis and conjecture. Whether couched in sensationalized headlines or not, the interest in Madoff as an individual "criminal" character was an element that cannot be disregarded in explaining how the story piqued the curiosity of an international audience.

Yet if the crime had involved only Madoff, it would have lacked the storytelling power which came with the almost epic family drama that also played out, a drama that the journalists and editors almost unanimously emphasized as one of the key reasons the Madoff case became a sensation. A father turned in by his own sons; a son who took his own life in macabre fashion; another son dying and estranged from his father; a woman at the center of the storm with serious questions about her complicity: Madoff's story was one with familiar narrative patterns and contours, one that was recognizable and deeply resonant in America and Britain. The Madoff family saga was in fact overtly linked to literary works by the media, whose coverage was riddled with allusions.

In the *New York Times* alone, allusions to works as diverse as *Julius Caesar*, *Agamemnon*, the tales of Charles Dickens, and *The Wizard of Oz* appeared.[16] Madoff whistleblower Harry Markopolos was thus transformed into Cassandra of Greek myth,[17] while several articles, such as "If Bernie Met Dante," alluded to *The Inferno* when referring to Madoff's betrayal of those who had invested with him, as well as to his potential punishment.[18] "A Jewish financier rips off millions of dollars devoted to memorializing the Holocaust—who could make this stuff up? Dickens, Balzac, Trollope and, for that matter, even Mel Brooks might be appalled."[19] More modern dramatic references surfaced as well. In the article entitled "The Madoffs Shared Much; Question Is How Much," the journalists note that "in the absence of direct answers [about Ruth Madoff's knowledge of the crime], all that's left is the sort of psychological puzzle that belongs in Act II of a David Mamet drama, right before we find out who are the players and who are the played."[20]

The London *Times*, the *Guardian*, and the *Sun*, too, found numerous parallels between Madoff and classical works of literature. Madoff is likened to Anthony Trollope's corrupt, mysterious financier Augustus Melmotte[21] from the novel *The Way We Live Now*, and to a Jekyll and Hyde figure.[22] As with the *New York Times*, both the *Guardian* and the *Sun* invoke Charles Dickens (but with greater frequency) as journalists present the connections between two stories, the fictional and the factual: "'He was immensely rich; a man of prodigious enterprise; a Midas without the ears, who turned all he touched to gold. He was in the City, necessarily. He was chairman of this, trustee of that, president of the other.' No, this is not Bernard Madoff . . . It is a description of Mr Merdle, the fictional banker in Charles Dickens' *Little Dorrit*. Madoff, like Merdle, was a pillar of the community."[23] Even Madoff's name was found remarkable for its Dickensian quality: "Bernard Madoff. It's pronounced 'made-off.' Could Dickens have named him better?"[24]

Reflecting what was found in the coverage itself, journalists often tied the Madoff case to epic tragedies in their explanations of why the case resonated with them. Anton Antonowicz of the British *Daily Mirror*, focusing on the family dynamics at play, asserted:

> It's a Greek tragedy. But how often do we feel sorry for the people who fall to the ground in the tragedy? Maybe there's always some sympathy. I mean, there's

obviously sympathy for the Madoff family in this . . . There's a suicide, there's a woman who's lost her child as a result of it, and so forth, which is, you know, very, very sad.

Four of my interviewees specifically invoked Shakespeare in their descriptions of why the Madoff story was so interesting and unusual. *New York Times* journalists Leslie Wayne and Diana Henriques, as well as Gary Silverman from the *Financial Times* and Ed Pilkington from the *Guardian*, each described the link between Madoff and the Bard. Wayne noted, "You also have the Shakespearean part where his son kills himself related to what the father did." Silver concurred: "There [were] very easily understood dramatic lines in the story . . . right out of Shakespeare." And Pilkington agreed:

> There was always a kind of Shakespearean thing . . . that you don't have to feel glee at his downfall to find it fascinating, you know—because he came from fairly modest beginnings, so to go from there, to rise to such heights and then, brung down to the clink . . .

Tapping deeply into the question of which stories have the ability to resonate with us as readers and indeed as humans, Diana Henriques of the *New York Times* said:

> Whether it's the Icarus Myth, whether it's Dr. Jekyll and Mr. Hyde, or whether it's Cinderella or a David and Goliath story, those are the kind of stories, I think, that latch onto our psyche—way deep down. Deeper down than simply the factual story. And this one did from day one, absolutely grabbed me from the minute I knew that he'd been turned in by his son. I said, "Oh man, wow." . . . We were thinking King Lear. It was Shakespearean in all its dimensions.

That these journalists were so unanimously and self-avowedly drawn to the literary, almost mythic quality of the Madoff case points to the centrality of storytelling in the news-making process, but also to the importance of having the contours of the story fit within already existing repertoires made available to us through shared histories and cultural traditions. If the facts then of the Madoff case *itself*, before it even entered print, presented themselves as fragments of a very recognizable story to the journalists, the mythic quality of that news story was only enhanced by its ability to serve as a tale that would offer "reassurance" through familiar explanations of complex phenomena.

Among the dramatic elements of the crime, the "character" of Ruth Madoff and the question of her complicity in the crimes was one that, unlike the suicide of Mark Madoff, which happened two years after his father's arrest, was present almost immediately and constituted a chief reason for public intrigue. This intrigue would continue long after Madoff was incarcerated, as evidenced in Ruth's fictionalized entry into popular culture through the Oscar-winning Woody Allen film *Blue Jasmine* (2013). Actress Cate Blanchett, portraying the Ruth Madoff character, noted in a *60 Minutes* interview that she had studied Ruth's own *60 Minutes* interview with Morley Safer in order to prepare for the performance.

John Marzulli of the *Daily News* described the public interest about Ruth which drove the coverage:

> I think it was sellable in the sense that people were wondering, what did she know? Here she was, portraying herself as the blind wife who was shocked just like everyone else, but I think that there was this great skepticism—probably to this day—as to how much she knew about what her husband was up to and how much she knew about the real Bernie Madoff.

Alexandra Frean of the London *Times* again invoked a drama—this time the HBO television show *The Sopranos*—to describe Ruth's story, revealing the extent to which the Madoff case was entangled in fictive worlds in the minds of the public and, perhaps, the journalists. One fascinating aspect of Frean's response stems from her use of the character Carmela as a way to talk about Ruth Madoff's guilt and Ruth's motives for wanting to conceal her husband's criminality:

> I can only imagine that she [Ruth Madoff] was like Carmela in *The Sopranos*; she probably did know but she didn't ever want to think about it . . . You know, Carmela was guilty as her husband in that respect, in that she decided to turn a blind eye.

While coverage of Ruth was prominent in the broadsheet/elite newspapers, the US tabloids, perhaps to appeal to a broader audience and further sensationalize an already dramatic story, went much further in their negative portrayal and in their assumption of her guilt. Take for example an article found in the *New York Post* by reporters Bruce Golding and Kavita Mokha, describing Ruth's visit to Metropolitan Correctional: "Ruth, 67, arrived about 20 minutes early to her scheduled 5 p.m. visit, hopping out of a *black* SUV. Clutching a *black* umbrella and clad in a long *black* coat with the hood up, she was accompanied by two security escorts who tried to block photographers as she headed for the lockup. With a smirk on her face, she ignored reporters' questions."[25] Ruth is symbolically here painted as a black, condescending, elitist figure standing apart from the masses without repentance and without any regard for those trying to get answers to the crime.

While less conjectural, sensationalized accounts of Ruth Madoff and her involvement in the crime were to be found in the coverage provided, say, by the *New York Times*, it is important to acknowledge how coverage of Ruth broadly functioned to enhance interest in the case. If, as Alexandra Frean implied, she is seen as a "Carmela Soprano," a very rich woman who closed her eyes to crime in order to benefit from it, then it is much easier for her to fall into a preexisting set of archetypal characters and therefore be familiar, able to be discussed by the public and brought into discourse.

James Doran, a British journalist who wrote for the *Guardian* as well as the *New York Post*, reflected on the coverage of Ruth:

> Well, frankly, we pushed it as far as we could because . . . I mean, she was his wife. If it had gone on for a few months, then perhaps she could have been duped . . . but you can't live with someone for all those years . . . He was an out-and-out criminal! . . . I should say so she knew. She was a kind of mall, frankly, in *New York Post* parlance. She just lived on the Upper East Side, that's all.

From prison, Bernie Madoff would continue to follow coverage of his case, reading the *Wall Street Journal* and *New York Times* on a daily basis. When I asked him about the media representation of his case, the coverage of his family and particularly his son Mark came to the surface. He described the portrayal of his sons, but also the way the paparazzi-like attention affected them:

> The media frenzy also covered my family, and my sons could not leave their houses . . . The most hurtful article concerned the funeral of my son Mark in the *NY Post* and other papers. The headlines shouted that BERNIE REFUSES TO ATTEND HIS SON'S FUNERAL. The sad fact was that the prison had told me that I could not get approval to attend for public safety reasons.

He would later add, "The constant media distortion and harassment has contributed to the death of my son and humiliation of my family."

A Swindle of Mythological Proportions

Even with its internal Shakespearean family dynamics, Madoff's Ponzi was not the only instance of significant fraud unrelated to the financial crisis that emerged during the economic free-fall. Among the most notable examples was Marc Dreier, a successful New York lawyer boasting a list of celebrity clientele, who was arrested in Canada in early December, only a week before the FBI arrived at Madoff's apartment. Dreier had stolen $400 million in a Ponzi, mostly from hedge funds through the sale of false promissory notes. The scam earned him the label of "Houdini" from prosecutor Jonathan Streeter,[26] as it entailed a series of film-worthy machinations including impersonations, phony web sites, forged documents, and fake statements issued to clients.[27] Ostentatious Texas billionaire and cricket aficionado Robert Allen Stanford was charged soon after in February 2009 for running a $7 billion Ponzi scheme that ensnared approximately twenty thousand victims, selling phony certificates of deposit, a crime which would later earn him a 110-year sentence.[28] And in Brooklyn, Philip Barry's Ponzi, a crime which spanned decades since the 1970s, also toppled in 2009, leaving hundreds of primarily working-class investors with losses at an estimated $24 million.[29]

While these cases did receive some media attention, it paled in comparison to that lavished on Madoff's fraud. Dreier's, Stanford's, and Barry's crimes—although comparisons were sometimes drawn with Madoff's—were not to become focal points for national and international discourse about the financial crisis. In a time when *trillions* were being lost (US stock market losses between 2007 and March 2009 were estimated around $12 trillion[30]), *millions* had lost its ability to grab the attention of a public inured to financial catastrophe. Before the daunting figure of the initially reported $65 billion lost in the Madoff scam, even Robert Allen Stanford's $7 billion in bilked funds could not compare. As John Marzulli, court reporter for the New York *Daily News*, lamented in our interview outside of the Federal Courthouse in Brooklyn,

> I think [Philip Barry's] Ponzi received less attention because of the Bernie Madoff case. Sad to say, at least in terms of media coverage, the Bernie Madoff case has really raised the bar on Ponzi cases; we're talking about a fraud that was in the tens of billions of dollars, so when somebody is arrested in a two-million-dollar Ponzi scheme, it seems like chump change.

The sheer scale of the fraud was the element most uniformly cited by those who covered the Madoff case in major publications as what made the case—in their experience as journalists—interesting, unusual, and phenomenal.

For example, in separate interviews, Tom Zambito (also a court reporter for the New York *Daily News*), Anton Antonowicz (of the British *Daily Mirror*), and Kaja Whitehouse (business reporter for the *New York Post*) described how the $65 billion loss was enough to bring this financial fraud case to the pages of tabloids typically uninterested in covering white-collar crime. The tabloid coverage transcended traditional class boundaries and led to a much broader cultural discourse. This particular white-collar crime not only appealed to the elite readerships of the London *Times* and the *New York Times*; it also resonated with lower-middle- and working-class people who were experiencing their own crisis-related hardship. Zambito reflected on the *Daily News*'s coverage:

> For the *Daily News*, that was not a specialty of ours—financial cases . . . There was a lot that went through that courthouse that we sort of ignored, other insider trading cases, unless they had facts that sort of bumped it into our realm . . . For the tabloids, it's not something you would have found, if the amount was smaller. If it was, say, 500,000 this wouldn't have gotten into the *Daily News* or *New York Post*. It would have been a B3 story in the *New York Times*.

Whitehouse described being struck by the story when it initially broke:

> The dollar figure . . . I mean, obviously it's been ratcheted down a lot, but there's never been anything like that—number-wise I think he came out and said fifty-five billion at first, and it's like, fifty-five *billion* dollars—crazy!

For the elite/broadsheet papers in both the United States and the United Kingdom, the sheer scale of the fraud was seen by journalists and editors as a once-in-a-lifetime, extraordinary story, even for audiences with ostensibly more financial sophistication and interest in reading about white-collar crime than their counterparts. The US deputy managing editor for the *Financial Times*, Gary Silverman, invoked a popular mystery writer in reaction, and drew attention to the amount's mythological dimension:

> It was the biggest case because it was the biggest number, and the thing that was amazing from the start was the number, the amount missing, that made it, in Agatha Christie terms, a giant crime.

The number was so large that Ed Pilkington (of the *Guardian*) was at first skeptical of the tens of billions in losses. By his account, even as he began to write about the scandal, he believed the number could not be correct: "In the first case it was just simply the scale that caught my eye," he remembered. "Just simply the scale—one person—the size of it just caught my eye. Wow."

At the *New York Times*'s high-rise building in Manhattan, Diana Henriques, the journalist perhaps most associated with coverage of the Madoff case, detailed the breathless first moments before the case broke:

> We went into work every day saying, "Will the ATMs still be working by night-fall?" It was *that* kind of crisis. So I had no way I could even pitch the story until I had some idea of what the scale was. So I called a regulatory source who was familiar with the case and he said, "I can't talk yet." I said, "You don't have to talk to me. Just—I want one clue, I want to know, what is the scale of this crime? Because, you know, we don't have space, frankly." It's 4:15 in the afternoon, we're all there—my boss was going to go in fifteen minutes and pitch our page-one

stories to the news desk. So I said, "We don't have room, we don't have time, I need to know how big the story is." And he said, "Huge." So okay, well, I hang up, told my boss about it. I said, "You know, all they're saying: it is a huge fraud." And then as soon as the story broke . . . we saw that Madoff himself had estimated the losses at fifty billion dollars. So it went on page one as the lead story of the paper that next day. And the scale of it, even in normal times, would have made it newsworthy; the scale of it even in these very abnormal times made it newsworthy.

Henriques's eloquent telling of these moments in the newsroom captures my contention that the amount of money in the Madoff scandal not only set it apart from other scandals; it also propelled it to the front page. It was the almost mythological sum (a sum even greater than Marc Dreier's $400 million in losses) that let the scandal rise above the already deafening "white noise" of the financial crisis and capture the public's attention across class lines and international boundaries. Ironically, there is an additional element of mythology or fiction to the reported loss figure. Since the initial $65 and $50 billion sums were reported—sums which included fictitious losses as well as actual losses in principle— actual losses to individual and institutional investors have been given as approximately $20 billion by Irving Picard, the bankruptcy lawyer acting as trustee of Madoff's company.[31] However, as the 2012 Government Accounting Office Report "Consumer Outcomes in the Madoff Liquidation Hearings" describes, most of these losses can be accounted for by gains to other Madoff victims who withdrew more in fictitious profits than they had initially invested and hence became "net winners." In fact, as Madoff is quick to point out, more individual and family accounts were "net winners" than "net losers." And although he himself originally gave a loss figure in the $50 billion range to the FBI upon his arrest, Madoff is now trying to have the official losses described in terms of "net" losses. He wrote from prison:

The NET loss figure was 2 billion. It is a well-established practice to report and refer to the Net figure not the Gross. When a mutual fund or any other market figure is reported they use the NET gain or loss. Every mutual fund surely has investors that lost money during its particular reporting period depending when they entered and exited that year. Nevertheless the fund's reported year's results reflect the NET full year's results, not those of a particular customer's results. Similarly when any hedge fund or investment manager refers to his performance they never refer to any individual's performance results. You notice that the GAO refers to the results of "customers as a GROUP"; Picard NEVER does.

Of course, not only does this account greatly minimize the losses of the "net losers"—individuals and institutions who lost more than they had originally invested, which *did* amount to almost $20 billion even if this meant that other victims gained, as opposed to Madoff himself—but it also disregards the loss of fictitious profits, which nevertheless had real repercussions for those who had counted on those funds.

Yet despite a certain disingenuousness on the part of Madoff, his reasoning does offer us at least one valuable insight: when we think about the ways that losses became so central to establishing the mythological proportions of the fraud, it becomes evident that including fictitious losses and failing to clarify the gains of the net winners distorted or inflated our estimates of the total loss. This distortion in turn was used to present a fraud of epic proportions in place of a more nuanced view.

Cult(ures) of Celebrity and the Allure of the Madoff Case

Beyond the mythologizing billions lost, the entanglement of A-list celebrities, popular cultural icons, and historical figures helped to propel the case into the realm of the mythological and better enabled the public to engage in discourse about the financial crisis. Over the last twenty years, cultural studies scholars and social scientists increasingly have looked closely at the "celebrity cultures" that have arisen in America and Britain,[32] and have provided useful research to frame the Madoff case. Cardiff University's Michael Levi, one of the few modern criminologists to write about media portrayals of white-collar crime, posits that the influence of the late-modern "cult of the celebrity" has forced media producers to focus on well-known figures in order to gain readership; so only cases which involve these persons will be extensively covered. Due to media's status as a source of entertainment, celebrity victims and offenders are "preferred" subjects.[33] Criminologist Robert Reiner remarks, "The fact/fiction distinction has become more fluid in recent years . . . The reporting of white collar crime tends to be concentrated in 'quality' newspapers and is often restricted to specialist financial pages, sections, or newspapers, framed in ways that mark it off from 'real' crime *unless* these are sensational celebrity-style stories that are treated as a form of 'infotainment.'"[34]

Certainly, then, the Madoff story was attractive for its infotainment properties. Each of the media sources used in this book's content analysis—be it left-leaning or right-leaning, tabloid or broadsheet, British or American—sprinkled celebrity liberally into its reportage. *Daily News* headlines included "Even Uma Beau Gets Skimmed,"[35] "Add Zsa Zsa to Growing List of Big Madoff Victims,"[36] and "He's 'Forrest Chump': H'wood Script Writer Sues Investment Mgr. for Losing Big Bucks in Ponzi Scheme."[37] Because of the international influence of Hollywood, UK newspapers often used the same high-profile names to highlight the significance of the fraud. Suzy Jaggers and Christine Seib of the London *Times* in their article "Tremors of Madoff Scandal Spread Wide as Bacon Is Caught Up in the Scandal" write, "Other apparent victims include Steven Spielberg, the film director, and Eric Roth, writer of *The Curious Case of Benjamin Button*, a new hit film that stars Brad Pitt."[38] There was no need of course to include that Eric Roth's new film was a hit starring Brad Pitt. But the inclusion of yet another celebrity name added to the magnetism of the article in a market where writers are constantly vying for an audience.

Several of my interviewees, primarily those writing for the tabloid newspapers, emphasized the attractiveness and the importance of the celebrity factor. *Daily Mail* writer Anton Antonowicz, in speaking about what caught his attention about the Madoff case, mentions:

> There was the showbiz angle: Steven Spielberg was supposed to have been involved and—Dennis Quaid or somebody like that [and] . . . Kevin Bacon!

For New York-based papers, the involvement of the Mets baseball team's owners—Fred Wilpon and Saul Katz—as dubious victims also held a strong appeal and connected to the principle of infotainment. Tellingly, the *New York Times* covered this aspect from the Sports Desk as well, demonstrating its appeal beyond the business pages. Serge Kovaleski of the *Times*, who did extensive investigative work on the Mets/Wilpon connection to Madoff, noted:

> I think it's safe to say that undoubtedly the coverage would have been less if it weren't the Mets, if [the Wilpons] were just sort of big successful real estate people. It would have been much different. Then, you had potentially to save . . . an entire major league baseball team, . . . I believe the major entertainment market in the country.

Kaja Whitehouse of the *New York Post* as well as Christina Boyle and John Marzulli of the *Daily News* also emphasized the significance to their readership of having the owners of the Mets—a sports team with "celebrity" status—ensnared in the Madoff Ponzi. Boyle commented:

> The *Daily News* is a big sport paper—Yankees, Mets . . . People are kind of fascinated by these people. They know their names, even if it's not their money. They're almost like celebrities to their sports fans.

Marzulli and Whitehouse both suggested that the Wilpons/Madoff story caught the attention of their readership due to preexisting negative feelings about the Wilpons and deeply held emotions concerning their team's ability, or lack thereof, to win. Marzulli observed:

> [There was a] public beating that the Wilpons took for the Mets's fortunes on the field, and the team has really been very disappointing . . . Some of that anger at the Wilpons and the Mets's fortunes . . . came out in the Madoff [case] . . . People were saying that this should be a good reason for them to sell the team . . . We should get new owners.

Whitehouse agreed that the sports team connection drew local New Yorkers even more to the story:

> It had resonance with the reader . . . Even a lot of Mets fans hate the Wilpons. So it was a hard story to cover, because people were very emotional . . . Sometimes, if I wrote a story that seemed to be pro-Wilpon, I would have Mets fans screaming at me.

For those in the United Kingdom, who obviously could not possess the same kind of fierce attachment to the Mets, more local celebrity ties were made. The *Sun* noted that "footie legend Paul McGrath" had also been impacted.[39] Importantly, too, there was the involvement of the nationally significant figure, Nicola Horlick. Horlick, an investment fund manager for Bramdean Alternatives and termed a "superwoman" by the UK press, lost twenty-one million pounds to Madoff. Stephen Foley and Tom Leonard, who wrote for the *Independent* and the *Daily Mail* respectively, concurred that the Madoff case would have had particular resonance for a British audience given the victimization of Horlick. Foley emphasized:

> It was Nicola Horlick's involvement . . . She's a famous household figure, so the minute you get a London connection suddenly you can get your stuff in the international media.

Leonard pointed out aspects of Horlick's personality that made her involvement in the Madoff scam especially appealing to a British audience:

> Nicola Horlick had been seen as kind of smug . . . She never puts her foot wrong financially . . . and she was being put out like the rest of them. So there was a certain schadenfreude there again with her, but yeah, she's famous in England and the fact she was taken in was definitely a factor.

None of the journalists and editors felt that the celebrity element—be it Hollywood celebrity or sports team involvement or a high-profile CEO—was a necessary precondition to the exiting of Madoff from the business pages and broadsheets into the mainstream. However, it cannot be discounted, especially for its ability to attract readers who otherwise would not have been impacted by the case or seen its immediate relevance for their own lives. Madoff, by conning celebrities, was simultaneously able to enter into a kind of pop-cultural consciousness of US and UK citizens, who in a sense share common celebrities due to the ubiquity of celebrity culture and shared language.

In fact, because of this nexus between Madoff and pop culture, he *himself* became a kind of criminal pseudocelebrity in a way analogous to that of famous serial and mass killers such as Ted Bundy or

Charles Manson. *Daily News* reporter Patrice O'Shaughnessy described the scene outside of the courthouse the day of Madoff's sentencing: "The metal police barriers outside the federal courthouse in Manhattan looked more like the gates at Neverland, with hordes of reporters from around the world . . . The King of Ponzi eclipsed even the King of Pop to draw a circus at his finale."[40] In 2010, over five thousand personal items, including the ironically prevalent statues of bulls owned by Madoff, were sold in the biggest U.S. Marshals Service auction in history, often for many times their value, to buyers expressing curiosity or a desire to seize a part of history. Madoff's piano sold for $42,000, and one of the centerpieces of the auction, Ruth Madoff's 10-carat diamond engagement ring, brought $550,000.[41] Even the most banal items—boxers, sweaters, stationery, a family dog bowl, books, ties—were quickly snatched up as memorabilia or oddity gifts. The frenzy witnessed at both his trial and the subsequent auctions indicates that the Madoff name had acquired a degree of celebrity "contagion" itself.[42] In other words, the items he owned had been imbued with an almost legendary quality by having been in the possession of a famous person, particularly if they were in close physical proximity to celebrity, as many of Madoff's items were. It was with some irony that a fraudster whose touch made money disappear now had the name fame that conferred value on quotidian items merely by virtue of his touch. With Richard Dreyfuss playing Madoff and Blythe Danner as Ruth in an ABC miniseries based on Brian Ross's *The Madoff Chronicles*,[43] as well as an HBO project starring Robert De Niro and Michelle Pfeiffer based on Diana Henriques's *Wizard of Lies* (in which Henriques appears as herself), the intertwining of celebrity with notoriety only deepened.

It Takes More than a Star

The appeal to a mass readership in a long list of celebrities, famous personages, and institutions, and indeed the growing celebrity and notoriety of Madoff himself, was undeniable. However, several of my interviewees insisted that what gave the story true pathos and allowed a wide audience of working-class and middle-class people to connect to it was not the victimization of the Steven Spielbergs or Sandy Koufaxes or John Malkoviches of the world, but the victimization of "everyday" and "Main Street" folks. Alexandra Frean of the London *Times* thought that the celebrity factor made the story "a bit more sexy," but "you're not going to feel sorry for the celebrities in the way that you feel sorry for the poor widow." Christina Boyle, who covered the Madoff case for the *Daily News*, actually went as far to say that *because* it wasn't only the celebrities of the world that were affected, her readership "in the boroughs, a lot of cops and firefighters, lower middle class" kept its interest in the Madoff case:

> None of the *Daily News* readers would have had money invested in Madoff . . . What was interesting was that the [victims were] generally people who were hardworking, self-made who had their lifesavings taken away . . . Everyone could relate to that. It wasn't just like it was Steven Spielberg's lifesavings. It was some person you've never heard of who has worked really hard in a law firm for thirty years and invested money in a trust fund for his kids and then that had been wiped away, so . . . I think that would probably appeal to *Daily News* readers because . . . it was just this kind of human aspect of what he'd done and your normal, ordinary people who had been ripped off and had had their whole lifesavings just wiped out.

Juxtaposing the bilking of "normal, ordinary people" with those in higher echelons contributed to the theme of social inequality in the case (discussed in Chapter 4), as it provided the ideal forum for discussions of class distinctions and greed during a time of crisis.

Fagin, Shylock ... Madoff?

The last element of the Madoff case that moved it from the business pages, created lasting intrigue, and stirred mass anger was the way Madoff's Jewishness fed into well-known stereotypes during a time when anti-Semitism was resurfacing. Since many of Madoff's victims were fellow Jews, the case also presented a fascinating narrative of "insider" betrayal within a historically persecuted ethnic group. As Michael Berkowitz notes in "The Madoff Paradox: American Jewish Sage, Savior, and Thief," he became a "lightning rod for another round of accusations associating Jews with financial crime and other nefarious deeds."[44] He goes on to conclude, if somewhat hyperbolically, "The damage he caused the Jewish community in the United States and worldwide is utterly unprecedented, far worse than the OPEC-led boycotts of Israel and the efforts of self-professed anti-Semites."

The connection between Madoff and anti-Semitism is complex. One the one hand, within broadsheet and tabloid publications there was very little explicit or overt anti-Semitism. At the same time, it was impossible to accurately report the case without also at least mentioning religious and cultural identity (since so many of Madoff's victims were part of the Jewish community, and since he used his own membership in this community to gain the trust of his marks). More disturbingly, as detailed below, the Madoff case developed at a time when there was an acute resurgence of anti-Jewish thought and was often greeted with blatantly anti-Semitic responses from readers and viewers. As I shall argue, in this context, it is naïve to think that the expansion of the Madoff case (into daily, front-page news) was not somehow connected to anti-Semitic thought within US and UK cultures.[45]

I described earlier the numerous literary allusions found in the coverage that tied the Madoff case to classic works of English and American literature, particularly to those of Charles Dickens and William Shakespeare. The familiarity of the dramatic elements, the archetypal characters, all contributed to the allurement of the story for a broad audience. Dickens and Shakespeare were also the creators of two very well known stereotypical Jewish characters: Fagin and Shylock. Shakespeare's Shylock from the *Merchant of Venice* (a play overflowing with anti-Semitic insinuations and implications) is a wealthy Jewish moneylender through whom the "fierce diabolism of the Jew is affirmed."[46] Dickens's villainous Fagin "the Jew" in *Oliver Twist* likewise became a stereotypical, "exaggerated and archetypal image of evil."[47]

In her article "Time to Bury Fagin," Julia Pascal (of the *Guardian*) writes of the British revival of the musical *Oliver!* and draws connections among canonical and widely known literary works (in this case, *Oliver Twist*), currently existent anti-Semitic stereotypes, and the Bernie

Madoff case: "Madoff, a Jew, is . . . accused of a fraud whose victims are predominantly Jewish charities and investors. Amid this scandal, it's a mistake to think that American Jews feel immune to the threat of antisemitism. But US Jews are not exposed to the constant low-level anti-Semitism that filters through British society. They aren't confronted with hook-nosed Jewish stereotypes on the subway posters. Unlike London street talk, New York slang does not use the word 'wej' for cash (spell it backwards)."[48]

Many of my interviewees who wrote for the broadsheets felt that the "Jewish dimension" was one of the most significant aspects of the story. Ed Pilkington of the *Guardian* recalled, "The big one was of course the fact that he was Jewish and the way that whole sort of Jewish angle— story—came welling up." James Bone, writing for the London *Times*, added:

> I think the way it was a particular—Jewish—subculture was interesting, and I re-
> member—I think the first story I wrote about the case—I rang up Elie Wiesel at
> home because the kind of spectacular nature of . . . you know, a Jewish financier
> ripping off the most famous living Holocaust survivor, was just too dramatic.

Gary Silverman of the *Financial Times* also noted, "I mean, how bad it could be. The guy was, you know, a Jewish man who was hustling."

I am not suggesting that there was a deliberate or conscious attempt on the part of the vast majority of journalists to support stereotypes and stoke the coals through their work on the Madoff case (although the American Jewish Committee has alleged excessive references to Madoff's Jewishness in the news reportage). In fact, as I shall document later, most journalists were adamant in their belief that Madoff's Jewishness qua Jewishness was not significant to the case, and that the reportage had done nothing to reinforce stereotypes. My content analysis supports their assertions, as it revealed only a few examples of canard-supporting re-portage or blatant overemphasis of Madoff's Jewishness—and these were rare occurrences. Donald Trump (who was accused of veiled anti-Semitic assertions and dog-whistle politics in the 2016 presidential election),[49] in a *Vanity Fair* piece entitled "Madoff's World," described Madoff as "a

Svengali for rich people," referring to the Jewish fictional character of Du Maurier's novel *Trilby*.[50] The *New York Post* headline, "Ponzi King Takes Chutzpah Crown: 'Anti-Semitism Victim' Bernie Begs for Mercy,"[51] and another article, "Madoff Mauled over 'Heir' Mail,"[52] which began with "What chutzpah!" offer a glimpse of that type of reportage.

Rather it is the prevalence of the stereotypes themselves—the implicit associations found in British and American *culture* broadly— that made Madoff's and his clients' Jewishness a salient feature. The nationally representative "Survey of American Attitudes towards Jews in America" showed that thirty-five million adults, about 15 percent of the population, held "unquestionably anti-Semitic" views.[53] The same survey of British adults showed an identical level of unquestionably anti-Semitic views for the year 2009. Beyond the 15 percent of Brits and Americans who held unquestionably anti-Semitic views between 2007 and 2009, an even larger percentage of those surveyed were shown to believe canards about Jewish people, such as "Jews have too much power in business"—a sentiment with which 20 percent of US respondents agreed in 2007—or "Jews control Wall Street," an idea with which 18 percent of US adults sided.

Given the economic and historical context of a crisis and recession, when politicians and the public were looking for scapegoats, the stereotype became even more significant. Thus the story fit well with stereotypical preconceptions, allowing it to become a familiar narrative, readily popularized. Almost exactly one month *before* Bernie Madoff's Ponzi was revealed, at the annual meeting of the Anti-Defamation League (ADL), national director Abraham Foxman would give an address, "Blaming the Jews: The Financial Crisis and Anti-Semitism," in which he described a rise in anti-Semitic hate mongering outside of the mainstream media, on the internet, resurrecting old stereotypes about Jews as having a vastly disproportionate influence in financial affairs, as being avaricious and grasping, as being a uniformly wealthy group, and as having become wealthy by leeching money from non-Jews.[54] A body of research conducted by the ADL on a yearly basis which gauges the prevalence of anti-Semitic beliefs also certainly confirms a significant rise of such beliefs during the time when the Madoff scandal broke.

It is in this context—one of financial uncertainty in two societies where almost one in five believed that "Jews control Wall Street" and "Jews have too much power in business"—that Bernie Madoff entered onto the stage. The ADL, following up on its statements in November 2008 regarding anti-Semitism and its connection to the financial crisis, described anew how the Bernard Madoff case produced "a dramatic upsurge in anti-Semitic comments . . . on some of the most popular newspaper sites, blogs, and message boards on the Internet. Most . . . tended to focus on alleged Jewish greed and thievery."[55] Additionally, researchers from Columbia and Stanford universities, Yoltam Margalit and Neil Malhotra, published findings in the *Boston Review* presenting the results of an extensive survey which explored Americans' responses to the financial crisis and the connection between these responses and anti-Jewish sentiment. Their results showed that 25 percent of non-Jewish Americans blamed Jews for the financial crisis, with another 38.4 percent claiming they were at least "a little to blame." They performed a further experiment to see how public sentiments about big business could be influenced by invoking Jewish stereotypes. They gave participants either one script mentioning that Madoff was Jewish and donated to Jewish charities, or another script which did not mention these religious affiliations at all. Those participants who received no information about his religious affiliation or that of institutions to which he donated were much less likely to oppose tax cuts to big business in general. Those who read a news story which contained his religious affiliation and philanthropic donations to Jewish charities were twice as likely to oppose tax cuts to big business.[56]

The Madoff case thus played into an extant stereotype and was interpreted through an anti-Semitic lens. Several of my interviewees, including Andrew Clark of the London *Times*, Diana Henriques of the *New York Times*, and Binyamin Appelbaum of the *Washington Post*, were asked if they had received any reader responses or feedback to their articles on Madoff. Clark remembered that the anti-Semitic comments needed to be "expunged" from the web site, while Appelbaum recalled:

> There's no question that generated a lot of anti-Semitic response. That was the
> clear fact and pattern . . . among a certain segment of our readership. This played

into anti-Semitic narratives for some people. It confirmed their twisted theory about the way the world works. So that was a fairly significant component to readers' response.

Henriques concurred:

This is the first white-collar crime I have ever written about where anti-Semitic comments on the web site were daily—at least towards the end of week—issues to be dealt with . . . And God knows, I've written about other Jewish white-collar criminals; it was not business as usual from that standpoint. I don't work in a field of journalism that is exposed to that kind of vicious rhetoric.

As I often found, Henriques's comments here are extremely illustrative. She shows us how anti-Semitic thought began to appear in a forum where it was previously unheard of. It is especially telling that although her writing had covered other Jewish white-collar criminals, it was not until Madoff (and the financial crisis) that blatant anti-Semitic comments were posted by readers.

While it is clear from both the personal experience of my interviewees as well as the data produced by the ADL that the Madoff story caught the readership's attention due to its playing into age-old stereotypes, there was a second aspect to the "Jewish dimension" that also would have piqued the interest of the readership: the "Shakespearean" or even biblical narrative of deep betrayal—a betrayal, in a sense, of one's own people, who of course had faced such severe betrayal and persecution from those *outside* the group that a betrayal of this scale coming from the *inside* was unthinkable. In addition, Madoff's crimes were seen by many within the Jewish diaspora as a betrayal of the fundamental values of Judaism. As such, there is an awful irony at work here: Madoff, in his betrayal of his marks, betrayed the core values of his faith; in so doing, Madoff became, in the words of one writer, "the anti-Semite's new Santa."[57]

The personal and charitable losses sustained by Holocaust survivor and Nobel Peace Prize winner Elie Wiesel—losses of $15.2 million— captured most vividly this betrayal. Playwright and Obie-winner Deb Margolin's 2010 play *Imagining Madoff* delved dramatically into these themes, originally through an imagined encounter and intense dialogue between Madoff and Elie Wiesel, wherein themes of faith, betrayal, and morality are probed. After Wiesel threatened to have his lawyers stop the production, calling it "obscene" for reasons not explicitly stated, Margolin replaced Wiesel's character with another, remarkably Wiesel-like character named Solomon Galkin, while still maintaining the central themes.

This angle and theme of betrayal is the one the majority of my interviewees viewed as the more significant in relation to Madoff's and his victims' Jewishness. Diana Henriques in fact thought it was "the scale of the betrayal that made [the story] go viral." James Bone of the London *Times* likewise thought the betrayal was an essential part of the appeal: "The kind of revictimization of the world's most famous living Holocaust victim is . . . a story which is way beyond a business page story."

From my interviewees the common assertion was that Madoff's Jewishness was a part of the story that could not have been downplayed or overlooked because his was an affinity fraud that relied on insider networks and trust. Whether he was Jewish or not was, in a sense, incidental. If he had been Catholic or Buddhist, the important factor was that he had manipulated those who had accepted him as one of their own, those who had placed their money and their faith in him. Ed Pilkington's response is illustrative:

> Here was a discriminated-against group, and it was discrimination against the group that caught them in what happened, because they turned in on themselves. They looked for help within the group because they were so used to being rejected by other people, and there was this guy who was one of them.

While I agree with those interviewees who made such claims—that one could not write about an affinity fraud such as Madoff's without describing the community which he targeted by virtue of belonging to that community—I think it extremely naïve to argue that the readership assigned a neutral value to his Jewish affiliation which did not impact the coverage in any way. Given the realities of existing anti-Semitic beliefs as evinced through the research of the ADL, Margalit and Malhotra, and the documented bigoted responses to the reportage, it is clear that the "Jewish" angle was significant beyond its descriptive properties.

• • •

Madoff may have been inaccurately designated by *Time* magazine as one of the top twenty-five people to blame for the financial crisis of 2008; his crime was a fallout of the crisis, not a cause. Yet the elements of his story propelled it from the "B pages" to the front pages, seizing international attention and anger. At the same time, its temporal synchronicity with the crisis allowed it to be conflated with and emblematic of that crisis. Because of these two intertwined developments, his case became a site on which contentious discourses could center. The pages that follow focus thematically on these discourses as they emerged from the media coverage itself and in my interviews. I will turn attention first to the issue of regulation in an age of neoliberalism and laissez-faire capitalism characterized by deregulation.

3 SLEEPING WATCHDOGS: BLAMING THE REGULATORS

> In today's regulatory environment, it's virtually impossible to violate rules . . . This is something the public really doesn't understand . . . It's impossible for you, . . . for a violation, to go undetected, certainly not for a considerable period of time.
>
> —Bernie Madoff, 2007 roundtable[1]

> When the markets are going well, everybody's happy, and when the markets do poorly everyone wants to blame the regulators. And that's always going to be the case.
>
> —John Nester, chief spokesperson at SEC, personal interview

THE YEAR 2008 had not been a red-letter one for the Securities and Exchange Commission. Even without the Madoff scandal it would not have escaped the financial crisis without criticism. The federal agency, entrusted with the protection of investors since its 1934 creation in the aftermath of the Great Crash of 1929, was lambasted in the media and by politicians for its perceived regulatory failures, as was its chairman, Christopher Cox. With Lehman Brothers' filing for bankruptcy under its watch in September 2008, not to mention the failure of Bear Stearns earlier that year, the SEC had become a useful political piñata. During the presidential campaign in September 2008, Republican candidate John McCain went on the offensive, proposing Cox's termination: "Mismanagement and greed became the operating standard while regulators were asleep at the switch . . . The chairman of the SEC . . . has betrayed the public's trust. If I were President today, I would fire him."[2] Democratic senator Jack Reed (D-RI), a member of the Banking Committee, was quoted by *Bloomberg*: "A lot of investors are looking at the SEC and saying, 'Where were you with respect to auction-rate securities? And where were you with the securitization of home mortgages?'"[3]

Only a few months later, Bernie Madoff's Ponzi scheme, which had been left to metastasize unimpeded for decades, unraveled—not because of SEC investigative work but because the cascade of client withdrawals could no longer be supported. Details were soon revealed that Madoff had come under (and had miraculously escaped) the SEC's radar as early as 1992, when Avellino and Bienes (an accounting firm that doubled as a feeder fund for Madoff's fraud) was shut down by the agency. The *Wall Street Journal* had identified Madoff then as "the money manager for two Florida accountants who illegally took in over $440 million in sale of unregistered securities . . . [promising] returns between 13.5% and 20%."[4] Shouldn't this have prompted an extensive inquiry into Madoff? But according to the SEC, the examiners were "inexperienced," and thus as its own public report admitted, "The result was a missed opportunity to uncover Madoff's Ponzi scheme 16 years before Madoff confessed."[5] And then, with much fanfare, the story emerged about whistleblower Harry Markopolos, who since 2000 had persistently pestered the SEC with strong quantitative evidence of Madoff's guilt. In total, Madoff's firm was investigated eight times by the SEC and the Financial Industry Regulatory Authority—without any discovery of the fraud.[6] The SEC was again quickly at the center of contentious debate as the Madoff case became a way for people across class boundaries and with varying levels of financial sophistication to discuss how the SEC had failed in this particular instance, and also a way to broach broader issues of regulation related to the financial crisis. The narrative of "SEC failure" or, in the case of some of the UK reportage, "US regulatory failure" was by far the most dominant narrative in the coverage of the Madoff case in both tabloid and broadsheet newspapers in the United States and the United Kingdom.

The way this discourse about regulation developed in the media coverage is revelatory. It helps us to understand how UK and US societies construct the problems that have arisen in free-market capitalism in the form it has assumed since the 1970s.

By restricting attributions of guilt for fraud to particular institutions like the SEC (or even more narrowly to individuals within these institutions, such as Christopher Cox or Meaghan Cheung, branch chief of the New York enforcement division), the coverage allowed for a tacit exculpation of larger, more systemic problems. Coverage also downplayed the culture of Wall Street as well as the wider Ponzi culture[7] (or as Paul Krugman terms it, the "Madoff Economy"[8]) found throughout US and UK societies. Most coverage, too, did not place the failure of the SEC in the Madoff case in its sociohistorical context, a preceding era of steady deregulation coupled with inadequate funding and staffing.

The message of the narrative therefore implied that the solution to preventing future frauds was to eradicate human ineptitude on the part of regulatory institutions. In a sense, this atomistic solution suggested that by monitoring the competency of individual regulators, we could rebuild confidence in the markets and find the solution to preventing future crises generally. Preservation of the system rather than its complete overhaul was assumed in the majority of the coverage and in all but a few of my interviewees' assessments.

"It is almost impossible to put too much blame on the SEC for what happened"

For the majority of the journalists and editors I interviewed, the regulatory failure of the SEC was perceived as one of the most newsworthy and strongest dimensions of the Madoff fraud story. Alexandra Frean of the London *Times* went so far as to cite the incompetence of the regulators as one of the top three elements of the story that made it interesting to her as a journalist. Andrew Clark, also of the London *Times*, pointed out in our interviews the numerous investigations by the SEC that did not yield any evidence of wrongdoing. His words were remarkably similar to those uttered by John McCain in reference to the SEC: "They were really asleep at the wheel." Erin Arvedlund, who penned the now famous *Barron's* 2001 article "Don't Ask, Don't Tell" which first called into question Madoff's returns, likewise called the SEC regulators "shiftless" and irresponsible in their protection of investors who had money with Madoff.

Binyamin Appelbaum of the *Washington Post* articulated eloquently and forcefully the major themes of the coverage in relation to regulation, as well as sentiments echoed by the other reporters:

My conclusion at the time, and to the present day, is that it is almost impossible to put too much blame on the SEC for what happened . . . This was as abysmal and unmitigated a failure by a regulatory agency as we have ever seen. The red flags were so obvious and numerous. The fact that the agency had not only been told that this had happened, but had opened an investigation and still failed to find it—to this day, it blows my mind; and the reasons for that failure, the reliance on documentation produced by the firm itself from the firm's own account . . . —such elementary failures of basic procedure. It just boggles the mind that this agency could have failed as comprehensively as it did . . . The fact that there are fraudsters on Wall Street comes as little surprise to anyone. The scale of this obviously made it stand out, but the details were in no way unique. What is in some respects more remarkable is that an agency that was for decades regarded as the model regulatory agency—as the best, most effective, most successful federal regulatory agency—should have fallen so far and so fast, to the point where it was no longer competent to perform the most basic functions of regulation . . . It's just an astonishing story in its own right and to me in many ways *a much more important story than the particulars of the Madoff fraud itself.*

This connects closely with the crux of this book. Appelbaum's assessment—that the erosion of the capabilities of the regulatory function of the SEC, its utter failure to detect a very blatant fraud, was a "much more important story than the particulars of the Madoff fraud itself"—supports my argument that the Madoff scandal became an ideal story through which issues that were relevant to the precipitation of the crisis could be indirectly discussed. Appelbaum, in keeping with this proxy conversation, extrapolates from the Madoff case to draw a broader conclusion about why Wall Street had become riddled with the kind of fraudulent behavior and ethical improprieties that produced the crisis.

Much of the coverage in the British and American newspapers closely followed this narrative, which claimed that Madoff's crime was due to the abysmal failure of the SEC. These accounts often blamed specific individuals or leaders within the agency. Furthermore, these accounts, implicitly or explicitly, often opined that the agency's failure in the case of Madoff was emblematic of the origins and development of the financial crisis.

Madoff and the SEC.
SOURCE: David Granlund. Reprinted with permission.

Political cartoonist Dave Granlund, whose work features in hundreds of US and international publications, appositely captured this narrative thread visually in his 2009 cartoon "Bernie Madoff and the SEC." The SEC here is depicted as a decidedly nonfierce "watchdog"—a nervous, silent Chihuahua—while Madoff makes off with a fifty-billion-dollar sack of loot, remarking, "Don't blame me ... blame your watchdog!"

As Granlund's cartoon implies, in some ways the SEC was presented in the tabloid, broadsheet, British, and American coverage as equally culpable or even *more* culpable than Madoff himself. Representative Gary Ackerman's (D-NY) scathing reprimand to the SEC during a 2009 hearing at the House Financial Services Committee was cited in the *New York Post*: "We thought the enemy is Mr. Madoff. I think it is you."[9] A *Washington Post* editorial by Richard Cohen criticized, "[The SEC] were also, in their own fumbling way, accessories to Madoff's crime,"[10] while a *New York Times* editorial pronounced, "All of us, not just Mr. Madoff's clients, are paying the price for the regulators' failure to do their job."[11] The sentence does *not* read, "All of us, not just Mr. Madoff's clients, are paying for Mr. Madoff's transgressions." At least within this passage, the blame sits rather squarely on the shoulders of those at the SEC. The *New York Times* quoted fraud victim Diane Peskin, who in her invective offers a nonempirical but accurate summarization of the coverage thus far: "*What is our government going to do for us* considering the SEC, who we pay to catch fraud, dropped the ball? . . . This man *and the SEC* has destroyed thousands of peoples' lives."[12]

According to the press, many of these problems boiled down to bureaucratic and governmental incompetence—at either the institutional or individual level. Acerbic headlines such as "Madoff, the Midas Who Made an Ass of Investors" (*Guardian*),[13] "Madoff Made Mockery of Feckless SEC" (*Daily News*),[14] "SEC Image Suffers in a String of Setbacks" (*New York Times*),[15] "SEC Failings Laid Bare as Madoff Tapes Come to Light" (London *Times*),[16] and "The Madoff Files: A Chronicle of SEC Failure"[17] underscore this narrative. Gary Silverman, deputy managing editor for the *Financial Times*, jested during our interview, "The Chris Cox SEC I think will be remembered for its failures, not its successes." Given the media coverage, this was quite the understatement.

There were, of course, myriad justifiable reasons for such harsh critiques of the agency, its staff, and leadership. The SEC's own office of investigations issued in 2009 a 477-page self-flagellating report appropriately titled "The Investigation of Failure of the SEC to Uncover Bernard Madoff's Ponzi Scheme," which traced the history of the SEC's interactions with Madoff. Among the conclusions reached was an open admission that numerous "red flags"—from private entities and funds, media coverage, and internal investigations—had been raised, as mentioned earlier, beginning in 1992. These red flags, the SEC acknowledged, "should have led to questions about whether Madoff was actually engaged in trading and should have led to a thorough examination and/or investigation of the possibility that Madoff was operating a Ponzi scheme."

Indeed, some of these red flags were as embarrassing as they were glaring. Madoff's auditor, Friehling and Horowitz, operated out of a tiny suburban office in New City, New York[18]—hardly what one would expect from an auditor dealing with an investment manager with billions under management. The media also had raised a red flag: Michael Ocrant of *MARHedge*, the hedge fund industry newsletter, ran an article titled "Madoff Tops Charts; Skeptics Ask How" in May 2001, while *Barron's* ran in the same month Erin Arvedlund's "Don't Ask, Don't Tell: Bernie Madoff Attracts Skeptics." Although writing independently, both Arvedlund and Ocrant, their writings oozing skepticism, called attention to the extraordinary consistency of the returns, year after year, regardless of market volatility. Ocrant for his part noted that "those who question the consistency include current and former traders, other money managers, consultants, quantitative analysts and fund-of-fund executives." He also pointed out that those he interviewed about the Madoff returns from this group of industry experts indicated that they had tried Madoff's alleged split strike conversion strategy without achieving Madoff's almost paranormal level of success. At the same time, Arvedlund called attention to Madoff's lack of transparency and obfuscation. For example, Madoff discouraged his clients from telling others that they were investing with him. In addition, he did not charge his feeder funds any fees for asset management; instead, he paid *them* fees for bringing him clients!

The SEC's report embarrassingly indicated the agency was well aware of the *MARHedge* and *Barron's* articles. Furthermore, the report revealed that an astounding five separate SEC investigations into Madoff had not led to any evidence of fraud, and yet "basic steps" were not taken to confirm Madoff's account of his own trading practices: "Madoff's efforts to conceal his fraudulent activities . . . would not have withstood any real scrutiny," they concluded.

The media seized on this report, as well as on the February 2009 congressional hearings (on the Madoff case), to bolster their claims of the SEC's ineptitude. These accounts often ridiculed the agency through comparisons with bungling, clumsy characters from popular fiction. The *Daily News* wrote, "Bernard Madoff said he could have been caught in 2003, but bumbling investigators acted like 'Lt. Columbo' and never asked the right questions." The *Guardian* focused on New York Democratic representative Gary Ackerman's testimony to the House Financial Services Committee: "[Ackerman] compared the SIPC[19] and the Securities and Exchange Commission to 'Keystone Cops' and said watchdog agencies had failed to watch out for anybody."[20] The *New York Post* even suggested that investigators had let Madoff slip through their fingers due to the inability of regulators to control their on-the-job consumption of pornography, per an article, "SEC Porn Again: Staff Spent Hours Surfing Sexxxy [*sic*] Sites at Work."[21]

The portrayal of SEC regulators as Columbos or Keystone Cops[22] could not have been more aptly complemented by the entrance into the Madoff story of the quirky, intense, and outspoken figure of Harry Markopolos, who made dogged attempts to expose Madoff's fraud nearly a decade before Madoff's sons turned him in. Markopolos, an investment officer for Rampart Investment Management, a firm in competition with Madoff's, first gave an eight-page submission in May 2000 to the Boston district office of the SEC. He offered two possible explanations for Madoff's market-defying returns. One, the returns were real but were not being achieved through a split strike conversion strategy, as Madoff claimed, but through another—presumably illegal—mechanism like front running. The second option: "The entire hedge fund is nothing more than a Ponzi scheme." As this submission did not produce real action, Markopolos followed it with another in 2001, the same time the *MARHedge* and *Barron's* articles went to print. Again in 2005 he sent the Boston district office a document certainly not lacking in bluntness, titled "The World's Largest Hedge Fund Is a Fraud," which made the case using no fewer than thirty identified red flags. Among these was Madoff's allegedly enormous volume of traded options which, if actually traded, made implausible his maintenance of a highly clandestine profile (for example, never putting his name as a fund manager on any literature generated either by himself or fund-of-funds that invested with him), and the impossibility of his 12 percent annual returns which had only seven down months in fifteen years.

Markopolos emerged in the coverage as a heroic David in an epic tale of individual smarts, common sense, and rationality versus the Goliath of a bloated, mindless bureaucracy letting fraudsters run amok. Alex Berenson of the *New York Times* reflected in our interview: "The apparent ineptitude of the SEC . . . with Harry Markopolos coming forward and saying *I tried to stop this!* The fact that these red flags raised apparently weren't pursued . . . —there were a number of elements that made it a great, great story."

Andrew Clark of the London *Times*, who interviewed Markopolos, described him:

> He's a very eccentric character. And some of the assertions that he made were peculiar. He said he was sleeping with a gun at various times because he thought that they would retaliate and such. I think any journalist has been approached on numerous occasions by eccentric people claiming that they have a great story, mostly conspiracy, and it's very easy to dismiss people.

Markopolos may have been eccentric and displayed signs of paranoia, but his story added gasoline to the anger against the SEC. His tale of repeatedly leading the SEC to Madoff and being ignored exemplified and personified institutional ineptitude in ways that no internal reports about the ignoring of red flags could possibly have done. A government agency of empty suits was the problem and it took an outsider—a math nerd determined to come in—to expose the rot inside. And Markopolos was not a quiet, diffident wonk. His criticisms were outspoken, sarcastic, biting—ideal sound bites. He was able to channel the frustration and the incredulity of those who could not comprehend how the SEC had dropped the ball through his testimony to the House Financial Services Committee, through interviews with the media, and later through his own book and a documentary based on the book, *Chasing Madoff.* The *New York Post* described Markopolos's biting testimony (which seemed to implicitly evoke scenes from the Keystone Cops): "The man who tried to warn federal regulators about Bernard Madoff's $50 billion Ponzi scheme told Congress yesterday that the Securities and Exchange Commission is a totally incompetent agency that 'roars like a lion and bites like a flea . . . If you flew the entire SEC staff to Boston, sat them in Fenway Park for the afternoon, they could not find first base.'" As reported by the *New York Times,* Markopolos criticized the SEC as "nonfunctional and, as witnessed by the Madoff scandal . . . harmful to our capital markets and harmful to our nation's reputation as a financial leader," and called its investigators "financially illiterate." The London *Times* quoted him thus: "The SEC had enough to get Madoff. I drew them pictures. I gave them a road map. I told them what questions to ask and who to phone."[23]

Through Markopolos's personal encounters with layers of SEC bureaucracy, the public was also able to put names and faces to those staff who had undermined him, bringing them out of anonymity. The *Daily News* and the *New York Post* presented Markopolos's case against Meaghan Cheung, the New York branch chief of the SEC. Larry McShane of the *Daily News* reported: "He was particularly harsh on [her] . . . saying she failed to understand the allegations and asked no questions. 'Her arrogance was highly unprofessional, given my understanding of her responsibility and mandate,' Markopolos said."[24] The *New York Post* also latched onto Cheung following Markopolos's statements. Its article "The SEC Watchdog Who Missed Madoff," which described her "tearful" reaction to the accusations leveled at her, included a paparazzi-style photo of her outside her apartment, juxtaposed with a photo of a tauntingly smiling Bernie Madoff.[25] The *New York Times*'s editorial writers in "The End of the Financial World as We Know It" reference Cheung's shortcomings, quoting from Markopolos: "Meaghan Cheung . . . investigated [my submission] but with no result that I am aware of. In my conversations with her, I did not believe that she had the derivatives or the mathematical background to understand the violations." The writers acerbically queried: "How does this happen? How can the person in charge of assessing Wall Street firms not have the tools to understand them? Is the SEC that inept? Perhaps, but the problem inside the commission is far worse—because inept people can be replaced. The problem is systemic."[26]

Following the news of his case closely from Butner Federal Correctional, Bernie Madoff was cognizant of the prevalence of SEC failure narratives and blame leveled at the agency; he became defensive of the SEC and rationalized why they had missed his fraud, while at the same time disparaging Harry Markopolos, a frequent target of his ire: "The SEC has taken so much heat because of me," he would acknowledge in a letter from prison, while also hinting that conflicts of interest existed due to the incestuous relationship between regulators and those they were entrusted to regulate:

> It was impossible for them to have believed that I of all people would have put both firm, my family and they themselves in this catastrophe. The fact that the so called self-acclaimed whistleblower Harry Markopolos subjected them to such ridicule is as pathetic as he is . . . I am more than ashamed that it was my reputation with those very regulators, established over my many years of industry service that made them hesitate to believe I was doing anything illegal.

When I asked him to directly comment on the media's portrayal of the SEC, he expressed the same resistance to criticizing the agency that had in effect kept his fraud on life support for decades.

> The portrayal of the SEC was unfair. The Trustee made constant claims of all the red flags. He had little understanding of the strategy and how the industry functioned . . . The SEC was also led down numerous blind alleys by [Markopolos], who claimed that I was front running. When the SEC did investigate this claim it became quite obvious that I was not doing this. Where the SEC failed was in the lack of experience in their examiners who never followed up on the Custody issue which was a basic audit procedure. The SEC suffers from a lack of funding that is crucial with today's complex markets.

Harry Markopolos *did* present front running as one of the possible explanations for Madoff's otherwise inexplicably consistent returns. However, he had also offered the SEC a second alternative explanation, noted earlier: that it was a Ponzi scheme. As the *New York Times*'s editorial board had asked rhetorically, how did it come to the point where the SEC's examiners would lack experience and thus not conduct a very basic auditing procedure (making sure the assets and securities clients thought were in Madoff's possession were actually there) that would have uncovered the fraud years earlier?[27] The narrative of regulatory incompetence in "missing" the Madoff fraud focused primarily on institutional or individual clumsiness, but this discourse did not treat the SEC as symptomatic of a much larger problem—thus allowing it to be isolated for surgical repair.

However, a variation on the SEC guilt narrative could be found in a smaller, more situated subset of the coverage. This coverage historically contextualized how the SEC could have descended to its current nadir. It pointed out the institutional and personal failures of the regulators, but also took a broader view of the trajectory of the agency and historical trends toward lowered funding—as mentioned by Madoff—and a more hands-off approach to regulation. The agency had failed, yes, but the SEC itself had *been* failed and rendered impotent due to ideological and political shifts away from strong regulation and revised funding "priorities." This important variation was absent from any of the tabloid publications and hence was unavailable to one of the largest portions of the population.

Background Check? The SEC in Context

The chief spokesperson for the Securities and Exchange Commission and its director of public affairs, John Nester, was not the type of stick-to-the-script administrator I had been expecting when I approached the interview. Appointed by Chairman Christopher Cox in 2006, this veteran of the agency had a dry sense of humor that seemed useful for someone having to confront a sometimes irate public. When I asked him to reflect on the coverage of the SEC's involvement in the Madoff case and any comments he may have received from the public, he noted that he personally had not received remarks (the officer of investor education would have received them); however, he was critical of what he perceived to be a reductionist press:

> We received comments in newspaper articles. They'd say, "I can't believe those idiots, they should all be fired" or whatever. You'd see those types of comments every time there was a development in the case. The media coverage is fairly simplistic. Somebody won, somebody lost, somebody died, somebody was

born—they are all simple storylines these days and so now you have a bad guy and the victims, you have the regulator who failed. In other words, it's all very simple. So you never saw any attention to the real mechanics of the fraud.

In terms of the "real mechanics" of the fraud, Nester mentioned that, for example, after the *Barron's* and *MARHedge* articles the SEC was pressured into launching an examination of Madoff, and investigators asked him for records, "a sample of paperwork [from] a couple of months that don't have any logic attached to them," according to Nester. Fulfilling this request would have tripped up someone engaged in a Ponzi scheme, or so the SEC investigators surmised. According to the reasoning of the SEC, someone guilty of running a Ponzi would not be able to produce the requisite evidence of having engaged in proper trading. However, as Nester went on to explain: "[Madoff] produced them. So no alarm bells go off . . . They look exactly authentic."

In our conversation, Madoff, supporting Nester's rationalizations, presented the workings of his scheme as much more sophisticated and calculatedly designed to elude regulators than the SEC's critics and the media acknowledged. He had established through many years in the market-making and trading business the social capital and platforms which Harry Markopolos would later call a "Potemkin Village for marketing purposes."[28] It also provided a facade for hiding the illegitimacy of his investment business.

The claims that [the regulators] were incompetent and at fault for failing to listen to [claims by Harry Markopolos and others] were not true. The best way to illustrate this is . . . to understand the details of the transactions themselves. Not only were the prices the same as those executed on the NYSE; the volume of trades that took place in the overall market would have been possible. No person other than myself and my assistant[29] were aware of the true amount of capital that I was supposed to be investing . . . As to the S&P Index options, they were all reported as being executed in the OTC market, which was where most of those customized options [were traded], which makes them nearly impossible to track, by anyone. Another important fact was that everyone . . . was well aware that my investment management business maintained clearing, custodian, and sub-custodian agreements with numerous major global banks and agent banks and depositories, and that we transacted billions of dollars of actual transactions with these parties. [They] all had active and substantial trading desks in equities and derivatives who were quite capable of handling these transactions for me. Lastly, everyone as well as the SEC were aware that [I] had developed an electronic trading platform in partnership with Goldman Sachs, Morgan Stanley, Citicorp, and Merrill Lynch. I led the SEC to believe that this platform could handle our global executions.

For all the smoke and mirrors presented by Madoff to impress, intimidate, and mislead investigators, John Nester gave a qualified admittance of some lapse in diligence:

> So now with the benefit of hindsight, the staff could have asked for the counterparties of those transactions that would have had to be gotten from the DTCC, the Depository Trust Clearing Corporation—[or] whatever it stands for. The decision was made not to because they would have filled a truck that *no one would have had time to look at*. It turns out the truck would have arrived empty. But back then it just didn't seem necessary.

While staying away from the language of deregulation, Nester's presentation of factors which had undercut the SEC's ability to successfully investigate the Madoff case gave a strong indication of the material impact of several decades of laissez-faire, neoliberal ideology on the agency, an ideology which regards regulation as a bureaucratic hindrance to market forces—in Nester's words, a "burden placed on the marketplace." Not only was the agency, beginning in the Reagan era, put into a stranglehold, but the squeeze happened precisely during a time when the SEC should have been dramatically empowered and its resources expanded. Markets and financial products were becoming increasingly complex and impenetrable to the uninitiated; the Glass-Steagall Act banning commercial banks from also partaking in investment activities had been overridden; and capital requirements had been lowered. Simultaneously, the sheer volume of material the SEC was responsible for policing had grown. In his book *The Cheating Culture*, which was written as an attempt to confront the corporate scandals and perceived pervasive dishonesty in the early 2000s, David Callahan noted the disconnect: "The [SEC]'s resources are paltry compared to its mandate. While the number of company reports filed with the SEC grew by 40 percent in the last half of the 1990s, staffing levels remained flat . . . In 2000, the SEC was only able to review 8 percent of financial statements filed by public companies . . . By some estimates, the SEC would need to quadruple the number of staff reviewing financial statements in order to review 30 to 25 percent of statements and achieve what it sees as an acceptable level of vigilance."[30]

As Madoff also had mentioned, the SEC, even after the titanic fallout of Enron and WorldCom (among others), had not seen a corresponding increase in funds that would be sufficient to ensure the protection of the millions of investors for whom the agency is at least nominally responsible. Nester, when asked whether there was a cultural resistance to regulation in the United States that made it difficult for the SEC to do its job, diplomatically and wryly answered:

> I think the agency is chronically underfunded . . . sometimes worse than others . . . [With] the WorldCom and Enron accounting debacles of the beginning of the 2000s, our budget did increase substantially . . . because it had substantially decreased for the ten years previous. Even today someone will say "their budget doubled in the first decade of the twenty-first century." And it did. But see, if I only made a penny and you doubled it to two pennies, I only have a penny more than I used to. Doubling off a small number is no real accomplishment.

Critics of the SEC doubtless would have been unsatisfied with these explanations. Certainly the SEC would not have required a large budget to check with the independent third party Depository Trust and Clearing Corporation (DTC) to verify Madoff's claim that he was clearing trades for his clients. In fact, SEC investigators had asked Madoff for his DTC account number during an investigation in 2006 with Meaghan Cheung and staff attorney Simona Suh, but they did not follow up. Madoff would later confess, "I thought it was the endgame, over," and was "astonished" at the lack of basic follow-up.[31] "It would have been easy for them to see . . . If you're looking at a Ponzi scheme, it's the first thing you do." Additionally, Madoff had been flagged as possibly being

engaged in criminal activity numerous times. For example, while on record with SEC officials, he had both lied and contradicted himself on
multiple occasions. Consequently, expending more resources on careful
follow-up was warranted and easily justified.

Yet, to use John Nester's term, the dominant narrative about the
SEC and Madoff was "simplistic." The hesitancy of regulators to pursue Madoff was symptomatic of broader historic deregulatory patterns.
There were numerous, telling examples of this reluctance: regulators
seemed to fear Madoff as a "very well connected, powerful person."
Madoff possessed an array of incestuous connections with regulators
and even served on an SEC advisory committee.[32] Regulators, citing
sensitivity, did not press Madoff for important information as these
queries could have been deemed inconvenient and would not have been
appreciated by those in the industry. Investigators often seemed unable
to keep up with rapid changes in the industry.

In contrast, the historically contextualized subset of coverage provided a narrative that did not try to excuse the SEC from responsibility
per se yet posited its failure as understandable only through an analysis
of broader trends. This narrative was so ancillary, however, that in the
entirety of the tabloid coverage, there is a single sentence that mentions
structural challenges the SEC confronted. The *New York Post* noted,
"Former SEC commissioner David Ruder said the SEC for years told
Congress a lack of resources crippled the agency."[33]

This subset of coverage presented the funding difficulties and movement toward soft-touch regulation as emblematic of a trend in under-
valuing the agency and its efforts. The subtle but persistent devaluation
severely hampered the SEC's ability to enforce laws. In an article analyzing the reasons for the fall of the SEC from a "once proud agency" to its
current troubled state, the *New York Times* presented the testimony of
former SEC chairman Arthur Levitt (1993–2001) to Congress. Although
this testimony, in most reports, was either ignored or eclipsed by the
more dramatic sound bites of Harry Markopolos, here we see both a
biting and eloquent critique of structural problems at the SEC and their
origins in the overall political economy of the time. Levitt was reported

as stating: "The enforcement division has been hamstrung by budget cuts and changes adopted by the SEC that make it harder to impose penalties on corporations, even when there has been egregious wrongdoing . . . The commission in recent years has handcuffed the inspection and enforcement division. The environment was not conducive to proactive enforcement activity."[34]

The *Washington Post* also critiqued the deregulatory trend under the leadership of Christopher Cox, a former White House staffer during the Reagan administration who was appointed chairperson of the SEC by President George W. Bush: "Although Cox speaks of staying calm in the face of financial turmoil, lawmakers across the political spectrum counter that this is actually another way of saying that his agency remained passive during the worst global financial crisis in decades. And they say that Cox's stewardship before this year—focusing on deregulation as the agency's staff shrank—laid the groundwork for the meltdown."[35]

In contrast to broadsheet "liberal" newspapers in the United States, journalists writing for the left-leaning British broadsheet the *Guardian* did not shy away from using more politically charged words like "neoliberalism" and "laissez-faire economics" to talk about the SEC's problems and their connections to broader historic, economic, and ideological shifts. The London *Times* used terms such as "laissez-faire economics" and "Gucci Capitalism" in their coverage. In no other papers were these terms invoked in *any* of the Madoff coverage and subsequent discussions about regulation, inequality, greed, or punishment. The willingness of British journalists writing for left-of-center broadsheets to employ these terms reflects a different sociopolitical reality. Unlike in the United States, in the United Kingdom there is a majority socialist political party which "forces class issues into popular culture . . . [It] keeps the language and issues of class alive in Britain."[36] While the *Guardian* ran an article titled "Obama Promises 'Adult Supervision' for Wall Street: Recent Scandals Blamed on Free-market Dogma,"[37] the US media did not present the SEC failures as the result of "free-market dogma." Discourse in the United States about the role of regulation appeared to be closed to competing narratives that might challenge free-market capitalism in its present manifestation (a period sometimes referenced as "casino capitalism," "disaster capitalism," "voodoo capitalism," "finance capitalism," or "cowboy capitalism").

In an article immediately following the revelation of Madoff's Ponzi in 2008, Andrew Clark of the *Guardian* wrote: "Guided by a laissez-faire economic philosophy, the [George W.] Bush administration has favoured a relatively light touch in its oversight of Wall Street. Critics wonder whether this has tipped towards an era of 'anything goes.'"[38] Clark would go on in a separate piece to emphasize: "While [George H.W. Bush] was renowned for prudence and caution, Bush Jr. adopted an aggressively neoliberal economic policy. Better-off Americans got more than $1.6 trillion in tax cuts. In a 2003 stunt now tinged with irony, federal agencies took a chainsaw to 9,000 pages of banking regulations. Bush's choice to police Wall Street was a former Republican congressmen and devout free marketeer, Christopher Cox. His [SEC]'s reluctant regulation failed to spot Bernard Madoff's 50bn fraud."[39]

In my interview with Clark, he agreed that regulatory failure was one of the most remarkable aspects of the Madoff story—that it was "scandalous"—yet he contextualized this assessment by underlining overall patterns of conduct at the agency. According to Clark, "There was some evidence that the SEC under the Bush era was applying such light-touch regulation that it didn't want to look far when its attention was brought to something by whistleblowers."

Other key journalists, when queried about whether the level of blame the SEC received in the coverage seemed appropriate, indicated that their sensibilities accorded with the historically contextualized narrative. In other words, they felt that the Madoff case was a part of a larger problem in regulation. Because these opinions are pivotal to our question and because they demonstrate a lamentable gap between the informed opinions of elite journalists and the general coverage that is available to readers, several examples follow.

Peter Henning, who contributed to DealBook for the *New York Times* and was a former senior attorney in the Division of Enforcement at the SEC until 1991, reflected on the blame the SEC had received:

Who should be blamed? You can say the SEC, but that's like blaming the bank or the insurance company. I really think the agency became frozen . . . They were so fearful of bringing cases and they had been attacked up until the financial crisis for too *much* regulation . . . You look at it in hindsight, and you go—this is just an abysmal failure. But I think it was a product of a viewpoint of the agency, that "we have to go softer, we have to go lighter, we can't be too aggressive," and so they deserve the blame, but when you talk about individuals, I understand at least how it happened.

Financial journalist Diana Henriques (*New York Times*) also spoke directly to this issue. According to her account of the past thirty years, even under Democratic presidents the US government has been unwilling to give "teeth" to the SEC. She also described how this was linked to the realities of funding that John Nester had discussed:

The SEC at the time was hanging on starvation rations for more than a decade. Bill Clinton wouldn't even meet with [the former chairman of the SEC]. I don't think they ever met. He didn't even think about the SEC . . . in the early nineties, the SEC had been moved onto the side as a less-than-relevant regulatory agency. The people who worked there knew it, the people who wrote their budgets knew it, the people they regulated knew it.

In addition, during our interview, Binyamin Appelbaum spoke critically about the tendency in his publication, the *Washington Post*, and the media broadly to frame stories about government regulators in an almost historic and political vacuum, thus allowing for the dominant narrative of microlevel SEC failure to proliferate. He reflected:

I think that sometimes [the frame that the problem lies in government] diminishes or displaces other questions. Like how did we reach a point on Wall Street where this type of conduct was considered acceptable? How did standards of conduct deteriorate, and the ability of investors to police the management of their investments? There were lots of structural issues that extended beyond the role of government [but] it was the case that government received the lion share of the coverage.

Madoff for his part offered two contrasting opinions, pre- and post-exposure of his Ponzi. During a roundtable in 2007, Madoff appeared to believe that current regulations were robust and sufficient. Although in retrospect his disingenuous statements seem like the height of irony, at the time he presented as an earnest enthusiast for the current "regulatory environment," commenting that it was "virtually impossible to violate rules, . . . impossible for a violation to go undetected, certainly not for a considerable period of time." Later on, after his incarceration, Madoff acknowledged his cognizance of the holes left in the regulatory environment, as well as the funding and personnel inadequacies, which he exploited in the maintenance of his Ponzi.

Removed from the exigency of keeping secret the massive fraud, from the profit motive, and from keeping up the guise of believing regulation to be effective and stringent, his opinion accorded with the more historically contextualized narrative of the SEC. Here Madoff has resumed his Cassandra role: "It seems that whenever I think I have nothing more to add about what is wrong with our markets and our regulatory structure, I think of something else. God knows why I am so possessed with this subject. Talk about the need to get another life." He would also write:

> If you want to blame someone [for the problems at the SEC], start with Alan Greenspan, who was the great advocate of deregulation and the theory that markets would regulate themselves. Prior to him becoming chairman of the Federal Reserve we retained him as a consultant and [were] well aware that as brilliant as he was, he had no clue about the industry and its practices. I am reminded of a conversation I had with Lori Richards, the director of compliance and inspections of the SEC after the Mutual Fund late trading scandal [of 2003]. Lori said "Bernie, who would have ever believed that mutual funds would commit such fraudulent practices. My God, they are the giants of the industry." So much for policing themselves.

It's Not Us, It's Them

Although journalists writing for British papers, like Andrew Clark, did raise structural concerns which may have impacted regulation in the Madoff case, there was also discourse within the British press that complemented the SEC failure narrative which, as Appelbaum had noted, was found in a preponderance of the coverage. This discourse suggested that the Madoff case (and by extrapolation the financial crisis) was indicative of problems localized within the United States and therefore could and should be resolved by some in-house cleaning.

There is no question that regulatory agencies in the United States, not an international body, bore responsibility to properly investigate Madoff. But as the Madoff case took on deeper metaphorical significance and became conflated with a crisis that had a harsh global impact—including in Britain, where their own Long Recession began in 2009—it was evident in the media coverage that there were competing discourses about just how much Madoff was specifically a US problem, a failure of US regulators. Two narratives were discernible through content analysis. The first emphasized the unique failure of regulation in the United States vis-à-vis other nations. In other words, it isolated the United States, making the "problem" of Madoff's Ponzi one that should be addressed almost exclusively in the United States. It was a quarantined occurrence due to bungling inspectors overseas. The contagion of billion-dollar Ponzis was therefore unlikely to emerge on the shores of Britain. And because it was contained, it was capable of being reformed either by replacement of management, through better rules, or by imposing greater efficiencies. This narrative correlated well with the view that the United States, at the epicenter of the financial crisis, was uniquely responsible for the US recession and that which followed in the United Kingdom. Even the way the British media chose to label the Madoff case gives evidence of a Madoff-as-American-problem narrative. The London *Times* in a June 2009 article referred to the case as the "American Madoff scandal" when "Madoff scandal" would have sufficed.[40] The inclusion, however, served to create an imagined boundary between regulatory conditions in the United States and those in the United Kingdom.

Sentiments expressed by prominent British personages like Nicola Horlick, celebrity British "superwoman" of the hedge fund world, whose firm Bramdean Asset Management had lost 9 percent of its assets to Madoff, likewise focused attention on US failure. Both the *Guardian* and the *Daily Mirror* used the same acerbic quote attributed to Horlick. She had complained in a statement to the BBC, "US regulators c[an] no longer be trusted. 'I think now it is very difficult for people to invest in things that are meant to be regulated in America, because they have fallen down on the job.'"[41] International investors, according to Horlick, would greatly reduce their chances of losses, such as those she experienced, by an avoidance of US investment products overseen by incompetent institutions.

The *Guardian* in its "Viewpoint" went further and explicitly connected Madoff with the crisis, denouncing both as products of pervasive US regulatory lapses. Again, there was no reference to capitalism as a transnational economic order which has resulted in global problems, nor the complicity of international institutions or fund managers. "The SEC's failure to spot anything amiss with Madoff's business is a further indictment of the light-touch US regulatory system that was one of the causes of the credit crisis in the first place."[42] The London *Times*'s Chris Ayres, in "At Last! Someone We Can Blame for Our Woes," gave voice to a similar perspective: "America's critics will argue that Mr. Madoff's alleged scam is more evidence that Wall Street is inherently corrupt and that the US economy has in effect been a pyramid scheme since the Reagan era . . . With the recent housing bubble, for example, the US Government was Madoff. The profits from buying and selling houses were funded by dodgy mortgages doled out by Freddie Mac and Fannie Mae and implicitly underwritten by Washington—even though it was clear that many were based on lies and would never be repaid. In that context a $50 billion rip-off seems almost trivial."[43]

Alexandra Frean, the US business editor for the London *Times*, discussed with me her thoughts on whether the British public saw the Madoff case as a particularly American problem, or whether the case was seen as having more international significance. She substantiated the existence of a sentiment among the British that would explain this narrative within the coverage of a distinctly American regulatory culpability for both Madoff and the crisis:

It was probably seen as an American thing . . . in Britain, we regarded the financial crisis as a product of American making. There was a lot of anti-Americanism. I mean, there is anyway, but there was at that time because this was seen as the problem that originated in the United States, and I think Madoff came to be seen as part of that problem . . . I do think that you can't really understand how cross people were in the UK at bankers in America. The whole subprime mortgage thing was seen as an American bankers' problem.

A second narrative, though, also competed within the British coverage and was corroborated by interviews with journalists. This repudiated the view that the United States was uniquely accountable for either the failure to detect Madoff or the financial crisis—it was not the sole locus of breakdown in regulation and financial malfeasance. In its focus on larger economic structures, the narrative was similar to that found in the historically contextualized US coverage in which the Madoff case was a symptom of a larger problem within free-market capitalism and the drive toward ever more laissez-faire policies. These policies, according to this discourse, should be evaluated by all governments when thinking of how to inoculate against such occurrences and more seismic disturbances to the global economic order. The United States was linked with the United Kingdom as sharing the same symptoms of breakdown, indicating a convergence in the political economy of the two nations born of the neoliberal turn during the Reagan-Thatcher era.

"Could it happen here?" a subheading in the *Guardian*'s "Madoff Scandal: Pyramids of Deceit: How Ponzi Schemes Work" queried, indicating that the question itself of whether Britain too could experience a "Madoff" had become significant and concerning to British readership.[44] The *Guardian* could of course have provided answers from a range of perspectives but elected to publish that of Steven Philippsohn, chairman of the Commercial Fraud Lawyers Association. He wrote, "London is just as big as New York as an international financial centre and just as likely to harbour Madoff-like characters. As the credit crunch bites, more and more problems will come to light."[45] In other words, the United Kingdom was not immune, however comforting such an answer might have been in the short term.

In its editorial "Bust Bankers," the right-leaning British tabloid the *Sun* pointedly criticized the narratives that presented the Madoff case and the financial crisis as an American problem and emphasized the anti-Americanism that Alexandra Frean described. In fact, it praised the American judicial system for quickly disposing of Madoff and others of his like (conveniently ignoring the lack of prosecutions for the crisis itself): "This crash isn't the result of innocent errors. It began *here and in America* as mortgage pyramid selling, and morphed into economic Armageddon . . . In America, justice has been swift. Shamed tycoons have been toppled or jailed. Some, like alleged mega-fraudster Bernard Madoff, face years behind bars . . . Blaming it all on the USA is a cop-out. It implies everyone here was blind or stupid—or both."[46] Perilous investments vehicles—the hallmarks of casino capitalism—were recognized as existing in the United Kingdom, with high levels of risk passed on in some instances in the form of collateralized debt obligations (CDOs) backed by subprime mortgages. Regulatory agencies on both sides of the Atlantic had inadequately protected investors.

The London *Times* editorial "Boards and Rewards" also did not let British regulators off the hook with the "cop-out" that the SEC was at fault. They presented a broader, historically contextualized account that incorporated cautious criticism of deregulation and implicated Britain's SEC analog, the Financial Services Authority. According to the piece, "Financial deregulation in the last two decades has had benefits . . . but it has had a crucial failing. Financial institutions have been allowed to take on greater risks while protected from the costs of failure . . . That dereliction is shared by the Financial Services Authority and other regulators, who failed utterly to recognise the risk to financial stability posed by complex financial products and an explosion of credit."[47]

Along similar lines, another *Times* editorial declared: "In examining the policy options on banking regulations that face the G20, one should not forget the contribution that the regulators made to the 2008 recession. British regulators failed to foresee the recession. The banks may have failed badly in their judgement of risk, but so did the regulators, including the Treasury, the Bank of England, and the Financial Services Authority."[48]

Several journalists writing for the UK newspapers expressed qualified agreement with this less America-centric narrative of regulatory guilt. Alexandra Frean of the *Times*, who had earlier described anti-Americanism in the British public and anger at American bankers, felt that there was a general shift in viewpoint once the immediacy of the events had passed, which allowed for a more nuanced interpretation.

"With time," she said, "I think people had a bit more perspective on it and we're seeing [that] we've tapped into something very modern in a lot of countries, including the UK."

My interview with Anton Antonowicz, journalist for the left-leaning tabloid the *Daily Mirror*, captured both a more expansive attribution of guilt, as well as a historically contextualized account:

> [The Madoff case] reflected what has happened in America through the preceding years, . . . the relaxation of regulatory bodies, whether the FDA or in this case the SEC. And to some extent that reflects something in England as well with the Serious Fraud Office.

While not connecting the SEC failure to historical shifts in regulation in England, Andrew Clark of the *Times* recognized common value orientations and trends in business practices in the United Kingdom that linked it to the United States:

> I think this was a case where regulation failed spectacularly and I think it was kind of a one-off in the sense that he got away with it for so long. But I think the UK has expressed some greed towards things as well, and we've had a lack of a transparent financial services industry . . . so there have been plenty of people who have done similar things, who were punishable as well.

Noteworthy about the responses of Frean, Antonowicz, and Clark is their resistance to presenting the failures of the regulatory system and level of greed in Britain as being of the same qualitative magnitude as that found in the United States. In other words, even among those who see systemic causes at work there is still a tendency to label the United States as exceptionally egregious. For our purposes this labeling is noteworthy because it suggests that even those who believe in macro explanations may at some level also hold to the view that the United States (and its regulatory scheme) is a partial cause of the Madoff scandal and the crisis (and consequent recessions). Although many of these sources acknowledged the parallelisms in the coverage and in their own opinions, a conflict is still evident between the competing narratives. This conflict impacts not only discussion of the Madoff case but also discussion of the financial crisis, its fallout, and what the solutions might be.

Easier to Imagine the End of the World?

As we have seen, competing narrative threads about the culpability of regulators in the United States for the Madoff crime also revealed schisms in thought about their responsibility for the financial crisis of 2007–9 through the process of conflation described in this book. On one side, there is the dominant discourse (which received a far greater share of publication space and hence public attention), which emphasized individual and institutional snafus, and coverage in the United Kingdom which portrayed the issue as hermetically sealed within national boundaries. On the other, are the secondary, "situated" narratives that historically contextualized the SEC's failures, focused on structural issues in modern capitalism, and saw these issues as transnational in scope. Predictably, these two broad narratives led to very different proposed "remedies" to the problems.

In general, the prescription offered by the American broadsheet press was one that followed logically from the perceived etiology: eradicate incompetent staff members, give more money to the agency to perform its policing function efficiently, and thereby restore the confidence in the system that had begun to falter. On the other hand, with the exception of a *New York Post* editorial (which I examine below), the tabloids did not offer many ideas on how to fix the problem of regulation. Notably, although different political leanings among the papers exist, most of the solutions uniformly included strong reactions against more regulation—or omitted mentioning this as an option—lest the cure to the ills that led to Madoff be worse than the disease. The current regulatory scheme *in theory* is effective, so the *laws* should be preserved, and in the wake of Madoff and the crisis attempts must be made to ensure that the laws are not only theoretical, but enacted to restore investor confidence and keep capitalism afloat.

A *New York Times* piece from December 2009 is emblematic of most of the broadsheet editorials in its claim that "the [SEC] urgently needs new leadership, more resources and high-level political backing to recover its role as Wall Street's top cop."[49] The *New York Post*'s editorial staff offered an analogous prognosis: "Indeed, as the Madoff case seems to indicate, Wall Street's biggest need is for smarter regulation—not necessarily more of it . . . A properly policed private sector is still remarkably better at creating wealth—and fixing its mistakes—than the sort of command economy that more and more pols in Washington seem to want. Provided, of course, that the government is competent with the oversight powers it already has."[50] The extensive reportage of the switch in leadership at the SEC to Mary Shapiro as chair and Robert Khuzami as director of the Division of Enforcement rang with optimism and implicitly suggested that literal and symbolic change at the helm might be just enough to bring competency to the agency.

Of the US newspapers, the *Washington Post* was most insistent in its presentation of discourse emphasizing that more regulation must not come about as a result of Madoff. Rather, more of that watchword of the neoliberal impulse—*efficiency*—would be necessary in regulation. In a strongly worded op-ed, Sebastian Mallaby wrote: "The scandal doesn't show that [the SEC] lacked the power to regulate; it shows that it failed to exercise it. Responding to this scandal with more regulation would be like thrusting more pills on a patient who refuses medication. If commission enforcers get a bigger budget and are treated with respect rather than being dissed . . . as an obstacle to markets, things may improve. But don't expect a fraud-free era to ensue."[51] Another *Washington Post* article, "For Hedge Funds, Biggest Fear Is More Regulation," quoted Chicago fund manager Rob Topping: "'Do I think there should be more regulation than there was a year ago? Yes. Do I fear it's going to be too much? Yes . . . What you don't want to do is run the risk of killing the entrepreneurial spirit that made this country great."[52] Even though, of course, he overlooks that this spirit run amok was bringing the country to its knees.

The metaphor of the US financial industry as a patient being forcibly medicated with regulation; the sentiment that more regulation would be a death knell to the very spirit of America: these are provocative statements suggesting a deep-rooted aversion to challenges to laissez-faire principles, given the prevalence of their appearance in the discourse. Through the lens of these editorials, calls for a stronger regulatory state become the equivalent of reactionary fear mongering. Again, in this view the anti–Wall Street sentiment that brewed as a result of Madoff and the crisis was dangerous. The masses, awakened to the financial legerdemains which had led us to this point of near collapse, according to the editorialists, possibly endangered the status quo with their destabilizing anger. "The present populist backlash may not end well . . . High-profile examples of unvarnished greed . . . ha[ve] spawned understandable anger that could veer into destructive retribution . . . If companies need to be rescued from 'the market,' why shouldn't Washington permanently run the market?" asked Robert Samuelson from the *Washington Post* in "American Capitalism Besieged."[53]

John Nester of the SEC echoed Samuelson's, Mallaby's, and Toppin's concern in equally dramatic language:

> If you always ask for that voluminous data [which the SEC decided not to ask of Madoff in its inquiries] for every counterparty . . . that is a burden that's placed on the marketplace. The counterparty might not appreciate it . . . If the SEC would require every transaction to be processed and sent to Washington, essentially, the whole system would gum up and cease like sand in the gears of a machine.

The British coverage of the Madoff case, although it did contain discourse suggesting that the failures of the SEC and US regulatory system were uniquely responsible for the crisis and for Madoff, offered a broader range of solutions than that found in the US media. There was discussion about fixing regulatory bodies, yes, in keeping with the dominant narrative of individual and institutional failures. The London *Times* for example noted in its editorial: "The regulatory system needs overhaul . . . Sir Ken Macdonald, Director of Public Prosecutions from 2003 to 2008, argues for the creation of a single regulatory authority to replace the Financial Services Authority and the Serious Fraud office. Sir Ken's proposal is timely. The failures of the banking system are not merely an economic problem. *They undermine public faith in the foundation of a liberal economy*: the network of rules within which market transactions take place."[54] We hear in these words the distinct threat raised (as it was in the United States) to free-market capitalism lest the unquestioning acceptance of its ideology begin to erode.

But also arising through the Madoff case was a forum for discussion in the British press that went beyond quick-fix solutions to crises of faith. Particularly in the left-leaning *Guardian* but also found in the London *Times* was a willingness to question the very ethos, value system, and culture of the current configuration of capitalism, while simultaneously shying away from radicalism. There still was a Thatcheresque "no alternative" to capitalism, but it could be rehabilitated. The *Times*, for example, ran an op-ed claiming "the problem is more pervasive than the alleged frau[d] of Bernard Madoff . . . The banking industry encouraged the diversion of resources and intellectual ingenuity into the creation of complex derivative products . . . The byproduct was a corporate culture in which rules were seen as a constraint to be overcome more than as an essential framework for protecting the public interest."[55] The *Times* also went far beyond this critique of corporate culture when it published "Goodbye Gucci," reflecting on the Reagan-Thatcher years which inaugurated casino capitalism: "It was an era in which the fundamental assumptions were that markets could self-regulate [and] governments should be *laissez faire* . . . No wonder regulators were too weak, bankers too powerful, check and balances not in place . . . Gucci capitalism was as lacking in real values . . . I believe that the conditions are in place for a new form of capitalism to arise from the debris—co-op capitalism, with co-operation, collaboration and collective interest at its core . . . An opportunity to join forces and push for a more supervised, more equitable, economic system: one that tends to fair rules, social justice and sustainability and reconnects the economy with what is right and just."[56] The *Guardian* in a similar manner used the Madoff case as an entrée into discussion about how the current British economy itself was like a "pyramid fraud," where corporate Britain would need to be like a "junkie coming off drugs" and become less wildly debt-dependent, thus changing the current avatar of capitalism: "This time it feels like something important has snapped. There is no going back. Once this phase of weaning companies off debt is complete, we will have to build an entirely different economy. Without artificial stimulants, companies and economies will be locked into lower rates of economic growth for years to come."[57]

The belief in the possibility of a kind of "compassionate capital-ism"[58] or "moral capitalism" arising like a phoenix from the ashes of a Hobbesian world order; the suggestion that corporate culture's aversion to regulation, rather than the shoddy enforcement of that regulation, was the problem; the identification of fundamental limits to free-market philosophy: these were not the prominent responses to the regulatory failures in the Madoff case, according to most media accounts, nor were they the concomitant failures that led to the financial crisis. Overall, however, the way financial regulation was discussed through the Madoff case during this time of crisis showed a resilient cultural adherence (perhaps even devotion) to free-market capitalism and neoliberalism without the need for revision, let alone radical rethinking. The regula-tory issues that precipitated the Madoff case and the crisis were curso-rily resolved by removing incompetent leaders, toughening up the "top cops," and flushing the agencies with more money. If "the whole system would gum up and cease like sand in the gears of a machine" through more regulation, as John Nester warned, there was the risk that entre-preneurial spirit itself would be squelched. The narrative implies that it is better to tinker around the edges with things as they are than question the integrity of the system as a whole, or the ethos driving that system.
Yet despite this appearance of unanimity, a nascent desire to break out of the neoliberal trap (and its deregulatory schemes) found articulation in some aspects of the discourse. These nascent aspects could be seen more strongly in the United Kingdom than in the United States (prob-ably because of previously discussed sociopolitical differences, as Brit-ain possesses a higher density of unions and a sociopolitical reality in which debates about socialism versus capitalism can occur). The Madoff case's ability to focus and stimulate discourse about class inequality and greed in a time of economic crisis in both countries—the subject of the next chapter—would further develop this theme of discontent with the status quo and raise the possibility of a white-collar crime serving as an epicenter for change.

4 IT'S HOW YOU'RE RICH THAT MATTERS: NARRATIVES OF THE HAVES, HAVE NOTS, AND HAVE LOTS

There seems to be more of an anti-rich people feeling than there used to be in America, and it's no longer that you're rich that matters, it's how you're rich that matters.

—Tom Leonard, US correspondent for the *Telegraph*, personal interview

Ressentiment involves a sour grapes pattern . . . In *ressentiment*, one condemns what one secretly craves; in rebellion, one condemns the craving itself.

—Robert Merton, sociologist

IN THE HEADY DAYS of the 1990s, during the period of remarkable economic recovery in the United States and United Kingdom following overlapping recessions at the start of the decade, class tensions and inequalities in wealth, income, and opportunities, although always present, were not as conspicuously salient as they would become in 2007. The stock market had entered into a long bullish period (the longest in recorded US history) that went uninterrupted until 2000. As in the 1980s, delirium had seized investors willing to dream about a New Economy where growth would be infinite and where capitalism had broken free of the cycles of boom and bust.[1] Growth in output, wealth creation, labor productivity, and investment and low inflation coupled with new exciting technologies led to an atmosphere of lofty expectations for the future of the economy that bordered on the manic. Indicators of equality did not improve during this time—in fact, the inequality that had begun widening in the 1970s[2] would continue to widen as CEOs, investment bankers, hedge fund managers, and financial consultants saw their incomes skyrocket while inequality in the two countries increased between those at the top and at the bottom. However, access to easy credit schemes for the working and middle class delayed the pinch. Private consumer debt increased through the 1990s, with 1995 marking the first

time US consumers used credit cards more than any other form of payment, being emboldened to loosen their wallets in these seemingly good
times. They wielded these to accumulate over $500 billion in debt.[3] In
the United States, even those consumers who were at a high risk of default were given access to and in many cases were deceived into entering
into subprime mortgages with duplicitous interest schemes to finance
their American Dream of buying a home.

The collapse of the housing market and global financial crisis
stripped away this copacetic veneer of boom times for all in dramatic
fashion. Within the first three quarters of 2008, household financial assets in both the United States and the United Kingdom had decreased
a full 8 percent in value, and housing assets were evaporating.[4] Unemployment in America soared to 10 percent, in Britain to 7.9 percent. And
although the unemployment rate in the United Kingdom was numeri-
cally lower than in the United States, it sustained a more severe crisis,
with output losses greater than any other recession since World War I.[5]
Measures of inequality during this time could scarcely be expected to
improve, and indeed by 2010, 10 percent of Americans owned 70 percent of the wealth, with a third of wealth being held by the top 1 percent.
In the United Kingdom, household wealth of the top 10 percent measured one hundred times greater than the poorest 10 percent.[6]

Unemployment, drops in income, longer working hours, debt, underwater mortgages, foreclosures, reduced benefits, food and energy
inflation, uncertainty about the future: the psychological and physical
stress of these consequences of the crisis on millions of lives[7] forced issues of social and economic inequality and greed to the forefront. This
was not the anonymous workings of the invisible hand of the market
which had caused the fallout; it was the deliberate actions of those
whom the Occupy movement of 2011 would classify as the "1%" in their
reckless attempts to accumulate profit. For those in the United States,
the idea of the American Dream itself—the deeply held belief that material success is achieved meritocratically through hard work—was being
exposed as fraudulent. As the Institute of Social Studies reported in "Inequality and Recession in Britain and the USA," "the bursting of the

bubble in 2007–09 exposed the institutional fragility of Wall Street and The City, massively leveraged, overexposed to risk and even criminality in high places."[8] If Madoff, who once was arguably one of the most successful money managers in history, with a sterling reputation even among philanthropies, was a fraud and his gains ill-gotten, then how many others were there on Wall Street like him who had not yet been discovered by a feckless SEC?

To say, as many have, that Bernie Madoff himself became a symbol of greed, while being somewhat accurate, imputes a one-dimensional meaning to the case that does not give sufficient weight to the discursive function it served as a site for narratives about class and capitalism in a time of deep uncertainty. Bernie Madoff's multibillion-dollar Ponzi easily became a story through which multiple discourses about inequality and greed could be expressed. In this chapter, I focus on three key aspects of the media coverage of the case which demonstrated the US and UK publics' awakening to the causes and consequences of inequality and the role of greed in producing the massive wealth of the "1%" in the neoliberal era. I present the reportage of the anger of the public and Madoff's victims as concentrating and in a sense displacing the general anger over responsibility for the crisis, but demonstrating also broad, growing class resentment and skepticism of wealth. The fall of Madoff therefore generated a feeling of schadenfreude among those who had never lived lavish lifestyles and who had pursued the American Dream honestly, but who were suffering under difficult economic conditions due to the wrongdoing of others. Next I explore how narratives of greed-run-amok flourished as part of the new suspicion of the wealthy, particularly in the UK coverage, which consciously played to stereotypes of greedy Americans. Even the Madoff victims, presented as mostly well-to-do, were intensely scrutinized in a strong "blame the victim" narrative. The implication was that they too came into their wealth dishonestly or by avarice, turning a blind eye in pursuit of profit. Madoff's victims, in this account, were thus all implicated in the greed that led to financial collapse and recession. Last, I discuss class issues which came to prominence in an unprecedented way through Madoff. The coverage broached topics typically left unexplored by the mainstream, like inequality and class-based treatment in the criminal justice systems. Class consciousness was being awakened; populist feelings were running high; and it was a time when challenges could be made to the existing structures of inequality as they had lost their taken-for-granted appearance. The Madoff case facilitated this growing level of awareness when wealth was being demystified—less something to aspire to and yearn for, and more an index of dishonesty.

Anger, the Fall, and Schadenfreude

The media in both the United States and the United Kingdom emphasized and described in vivid terms the collective and individual anger elicited through the Madoff case. Words like "rage/outrage," "fury/furious," "hated," "anger," "seethe," "savage," and phrases like "seeing red" and "mob vengeance" peppered the coverage—elite/broadsheet and tabloid alike. By calling attention to this redundant use (or emphasis) in the reportage, I am not suggesting that real anger did not exist, or that this was hyperbolic sensationalism on the part of the journalists. I am, however, suggesting that this choice of vocabulary is semantically significant. It lasers our attention on that "mob rage," on the existence of already percolating wrath, and also bespeaks a generalized populist threat to the status quo, which if not contained, rechanneled, and neutralized could become disruptive to the current social and economic order.

Predictably, a good deal of the anger was directed at Bernie Madoff himself. A *New York Post* front-page headline pronounced him the "Most Hated Man in New York,"[9] while the *Daily News* widened the scope of the hatred, dubbing him "the most hated man in America,"[10] "hated by thousands, if not millions, around the world."[11] Anger against Madoff as an individual was especially prominent in the reportage covering victims' presence at his courthouse appearances, which offered them the chance to speak about their losses and emotions. The descriptions of the victims' anger portray it almost as feral, ready to escape the boundaries of civil society and enact justice vigilante-style. They were a mob looking to hang the transgressor, with the tacit approval of onlook-ers. The *New York Times* would quote an expert on sentencing law, Ohio State University law professor Douglas Berman, who expressed this ret-ributionist impulse: "This is blood lust . . . but it's a setting in which if ever a blood lust was justified, this was it . . . [Madoff] truly is, for lack of a better term, the Adolf Hitler of white-collar crime."[12] Interestingly, this public outrage became a potential card in Madoff's defense. For ex-ample, Madoff's attorney, Ira Lee Sorkin, would use the evident "blood lust" as reported in the *New York Post, New York Times, Daily News,* and *London Times* to make the claim that "mob vengeance" was being sought by the victims and these base impulses should not be indulged when Judge Denny Chin rendered his sentence.[13]

The scene playing out in the streets surrounding the courthouse was indeed portrayed as one in which the possibility of mob behavior needed to be tightly controlled. "Many of the victims were brimming with anger at Mr. Madoff," the *New York Times* observed, while the *Daily News* wrote, "[Madoff] will have to wade through a steel ring of police and private security guards in place to protect him from investors who want to *tear him apart*" (emphasis here and in the following quotes are mine).[14] The *Washington Post* presented a similar portrait: "On a clear but bitterly cold morning outside U.S. District Court, they wanted more answers . . . They wanted to tell the judge to show no mercy. They wanted to *vent their rage*."[15] "To his victims, Bernard Madoff is a mon-ster, a bastard, a psychopath, a lowlife, a scoundrel and a devil. The sheer force of the fury and frustration levelled at Wall Street's most notorious fraudster has been documented in scores of letters describing wrecked lives, plundered retirement accounts, families in tatters and scattered dreams," the *Guardian* reported.[16]

The portrayal of an image of vigilantism at the breaking point was enhanced through depictions of the victims' rallies outside of Madoff's Upper East Side apartment. One of his victims, in her expression of "blood lust," was quoted by the *Daily News*: "They should have him drawn and quartered right here."[17] The UK's *Daily Mail* described a sim-ilar scene bordering on mayhem: "The hatred was so intense that you could almost reach out and touch it. *A baying mob* had gathered on the street to hurl abuse, and one furious financial trader brandished a giant poster towards the window of a 12th floor penthouse apartment . . . Printed in bold black and red lettering, its message was all too clear: 'Bernie, it's not too late to do the right thing—JUMP!'"[18]

Fury over the crime was not limited to its mastermind. Although they were never charged with involvement in the crime and vehemently denied any knowledge of the Ponzi, Madoff's sons, Mark and Andrew, and particularly his wife of fifty years, Ruth, were described as being at the receiving end of much anger and scorn for their complicity, stupidity, or both. The *New York Times* assessed, "The public reaction to Mrs. Madoff has been *white hot* and vitriolic,"[19] and termed her "the most vilified spouse of a financial rogue in history . . . , pilloried and turned into a pariah."[20] Banned from her hair salon, Ruth was a "hated figure" like her husband, the *Daily News* claimed.[21] This sentiment spilled over in the courtroom, where as the *Guardian* described, "The anger . . . was palpable . . . [when Madoff's lawyer, Ira Sorkin] mentioned that [Ruth] had hired guards to monitor her husband's home detention 'at her own expense' . . . There was outraged laughter from victims who regard her money as ill-gotten proceeds from her husband's fraud."[22] In this article, within the space of a few sentences, the emotion is mentioned twice— first "palpable anger" and then "outraged laughter."

Given the feckless portrayal of the SEC in the media, as documented in Chapter 3, that the institution too would become a target of virulent rage is predictable. Joe Nocera of the *New York Times* noted, "Indeed, what you discover when you talk to victims is that they harbor an anger toward the SEC that is *as deep or deeper than the anger* they feel toward Mr. Madoff."[23] In "Waiting to See Madoff, an Angry Crowd Is Disappointed," Zachary Kouwe of the *New York Times* wrote that after the verdict "[the victims'] anger had shifted from Mr. Madoff's actions to the Securities and Exchange Commission, which they criticized for missing the warning signs of the fraud."[24] The *Daily News* also focused on the shift of anger away from Madoff: "Victims of Madoff's $50 billion Ponzi scheme have another target for their anger: The Securities and Exchange

Commission confessed yesterday it blew chance after chance."[25] Politicians, taking their cue from the victims and the public, became a sympathetic echo chamber for these sentiments. Their responses were delineated in similar terms to that of the "mob" in the coverage. The *New York Times*, for example, reported, "Securities regulators could not cool the *white-hot* fury . . . over their failure to act on tips."[26] Tom Zambito and Doug Feiden of the *Daily News* wrote of the House committee meeting on the SEC's failure to catch Madoff, quoting Democratic representative Carolyn Maloney: "'Many of us have lost confidence in the SEC.' She joined a chorus of angry lawmakers who howled about chronic regulatory failures."[27]

This discourse presenting repeatedly the raw, hostile emotions from victims, the public, and politicians—fury, outrage boiling over—was not merely evidence of a collective anger against Madoff as a result of fraudulent behavior and large losses incurred. After all, the vast majority of the public was, as sociologist Svend Ranulf, author of *Moral Indignation and Middle Class Psychology*, termed them, "disinterested." By disinterested, Ranulf means that for them there was "no direct personal advantage achieved by the act of punishing a person who injured a third party."[28] Most had no skin in the game, were not personally affected. Instead the anger was a manifestation of growing class resentments tied to the inequality and greed evinced so flagrantly during the crisis. The London *Times* observed that "the public are angry *and the media is on their side*. Initially this anger was directed towards bankers, but it will soon be directed at big business more generally: at companies that pay their executives millions while sacking workers; at companies that make significant profits but don't share the bounty with customers who are finding it tough."[29]

With this resentment there was a corresponding antipathy toward the accoutrements of conspicuous consumption, a concept first developed by Thorstein Veblen during the "gilded age" of the 1800s.[30] The laxity of regulations, morally dubious business practices, and criminality that were being daily exposed made such signifiers of wealth suspect, as questionably procured through practices that unfairly benefited the upper echelons to the disadvantage of the struggling middle and working class. *New York Times* journalist Alessandra Stanley appositely chose the phrase "pecuniary trespass" to describe the extravagant expenditures that in the climate of the financial crisis were perceived, by the public, as being sinful in their brazenness and profligacy.[31] The Madoffs' pecuniary trespasses—their multiple homes, belongings, champagne-taste habits—became the objects of interest, anger, and resentment not only because they were financed through fraud, but because they also opened a window on those Wall Street "types" who were bilking ordinary citizens. The *Times* wrote of Ruth Madoff, "[She] is viewed as an unrepentant beneficiary of ill-gotten wealth, *a petite and well-dressed embodiment of the collective, bloated greed that helped topple the stock market and the housing industry.*"[32]

The US and UK media, elite and tabloid, all lavished attention on the behind-the-scenes of the Madoff family's lives and presented in great detail their expenditures. Price tags were dropped, and adjectives heaped on possessions with novelesque embellishment. Mentions of Madoff's Upper East Side apartment almost always included the descriptives "penthouse," "luxury," "lavish," or its appraised value of seven million dollars. The *Sun* reported: "There is [Madoff's] luxury penthouse apartment, a 4,000 square-foot duplex, in New York's Manhattan. It has four fireplaces and a wraparound terrace. The kitchen has marble and steel tops with Baccarat crystal glasses in the cabinets."[33] The *New York Times* noted Bernie's penchant for high-end-clothing shopping sprees: "The last time he was [at the Palm Beach store "Trillion"] he fell for a $2000 pair of worsted spun cashmere pants, which . . . had to be ordered from Italy."[34] The London *Times* similarly painted vividly an elitist, privileged image: "[He commuted] from his Long Island home to The Street in a helicopter . . . With homes in New York and Florida, Mr. Madoff enjoyed the trappings of a wealthy New York financier . . . The elite Palm Beach Country Club, private dining societies, [he] played golf and drank with the exclusive tranche of American money for 50 years. His [offices] were adorned with Roy Lichtenstein prints and the glass lobby was with a colonnade of red granite pillars."[35]

The use of lists to itemize and monetize the Madoffs' possessions keenly demonstrated the fascination with and resentment of the insignia of wealth that went beyond the fraudulent origins of those items.[36] The *Daily News* and *New York Post* in the United States, as well as the *Guardian* in the United Kingdom, made use of such lists—either at the end of an article about the Madoffs or as stand-alone pieces. The *Daily News* titled one list "The high-living highlights,"[37] and the *Guardian* made a top-five list of swank Madoff items that would later be auctioned.[38] The *New York Post* tallied a long list of fifteen former assets under the heading "Ponzi-scum Bernie Madoff Stole $65 Billion and Wife Ruth Ended Up with This Golden Nest Egg of Assets," including as bullet points: "* 2006 Leopard yacht worth $7M * Boot slip for boat "Bull" in France, valued at $1.5M * "Sitting Bull" boat in Montauk worth $320,000 * Small boat in Florida worth $25,000 * Cap d'Antibes, France bungalow valued at $1M * $2,624,340 in jewelry * $39,000 Steinway piano * $65,000 in silverware . . . TOTAL: $93M."[39]

Clearly, as *New York Times* journalist Alex Berenson noted in our interview, "There was some lifestyle porn, people wanted him to be richer and living richer than he was." James Doran, who wrote for UK as well as US publications, agreed:

> There was [class resentment]. That's the whole beauty of the story . . . It was a sort of lifting of the veil on the wealthy . . . It's like, it's all stolen, to be a bit Marxist. These people were living the high life, but they were just thieves. They stole the high life.

Christina Boyle, who visited the Madoff's apartment for her reportage with the *Daily News*, described in our interview the public interest in Madoff's goods as "voyeuristic; it was being able to see inside of what he had and what his taste was like." For Boyle, though, the experience of the Madoff apartment was not one of being dazzled by opulence:

> It was like just going up through the keyhole into someone's life . . . He had the most bizarre things: I remember him having a wooden duck; they had their four-poster bed but it had the linens on it and it looked very dated. It was— floral-y, whereas I think you imagine that if someone has that kind of money

that everything's slick, but it wasn't at all. It was very homey, it kind of belonged in a country house. The paintings they had—I would never have bought any of those things; it was really tacky and tasteless. You're just intrigued to know: what do you do with that kind of money? You have all the money in the world!

The media's presentation of Madoff's lifestyle avoided any terms like "homey" or "outdated" or descriptions that would imply moderation. For the Madoff case to become the ideal story through which class resentment and issues of income inequality could be discussed, Madoff himself had to be caricatured—made to be "living richer than he was," his life presented as unimaginably luxurious, his money decadently spent on all the trappings, even though, as Diana Henriques pointed out,

by hedge fund standards, he lived a very modest life. He never attracted attention for his lifestyle. No one ever thought his lifestyle was outrageous or excessive until after he was arrested. I mean, he was operating in a world where Stevie Cohen had a custom-designed 737 with a nursery on board for his child.

That owning a 737 jet was the standard by which conspicuous manifestations of wealth should be measured in the 2000s is telling in itself. Yet those working- and middle-class members of the public who had taken a hit during the crisis could not be expected to think of the Madoffs with their multiple homes, yachts, private jet, and approximately 800 million dollars in total assets[40] as comparatively frugal. Along with feelings of class resentment, the coverage also presented narratives which elicited strong feelings of schadenfreude, of pleasure at the Madoffs' dramatic fall from grace—from riches to rags, from prominence to infamy. The schadenfreude can be seen as providing a sense of vindication, of just deserts for grotesque inequalities and divisions between the very wealthy and everyone else.

The New York Post published one of the most dramatic visual examples of how the media coverage attempted to satisfy its readership with a story of the unjustly wealthy losing their status. On June 5, 2009, a photograph of Ruth Madoff appeared in the New York Post accompanying the article "The Ruth Hurts" by Bruce Golding. The piece sarcastically opened, "Poor Ruthie, she's been reduced to riding the subway."[41] Ruth

Ruth Alpern Madoff, wife of Bernie Madoff, on the F train.

Madoff had been photographed on the F train in Manhattan, while behind her, with an almost too-well-orchestrated irony, reads a bright-red advertisement: "99¢ Does More." In my interview with photographer Caitlin Thorne Hersey, who had captured the image after being tipped off to Ruth's entering the subway by a *Post* employee, I asked her to take me through the "story" behind the photo. She described her ambivalence about following Ruth to take the photos and how those moments in which she encountered Ruth had created a "visceral emotional memory" full of anxiety—almost traumatic. A studio photographer, this was the first time she had to attempt a paparazzi-style "ambush" on a public figure, and she wasn't sure of the parameters. As she took the photos Ruth told her, "You're ruining my life," and berated her for what she was doing. Hersey exited the train to discover Ruth also had the same stop, and she continued to chastise Hersey on the elevator. Although Hersey could have followed her (and probably would have earned more money-making shots doing so), she did not. She explained that because she didn't know whether Ruth was complicit or not she felt wrong about hounding someone who was potentially innocent: "How could I live with myself?" she queried. "The ethics were so wishy-washy . . . This is not the job I do." Her editors had a different attitude. They were, according to Hersey, "tickled pink" by the shot, "totally psyched." In her anxiety to just finish the job she found so distasteful, Hersey hadn't even noticed the sign behind Ruth's head. This was pointed out to her only later.

Hersey's individual qualms about the ethics of her now-famous photo aside, this visual juxtaposing of Ruth—former Manhattan and Palm Beach socialite—and a sign of her having descended to the ranks of the average, was repeated again and again through the written coverage. The *New York Times*, for example, wrote, "She no longer goes to her gym, Equinox, one block south of her penthouse, where she paid $1200 a month for membership."[42] The *New York Post* smugly reported: "The formerly monied Manhattan matron . . . bunks with relatives and apparently does God's work, delivering meals to the homebound . . . The former billionaire's wife has been reduced to driving around in a 14-year-old clunker, with a parking placard in the back seat that reads, 'homebound delivery volunteer driver.'"[43] Even in Britain, the *Daily*

Mail ran "From High Life to Household Chores" featuring a paparazzi-style photo of Ruth bringing out the garbage. "As the glamorous wife of a multimillionaire, she lived the high life for long enough. But with husband Bernard Madoff in jail for a $65 billion swindle, wife Ruth has to get used to a life far less lavish than the one she once enjoyed," the article recounted, describing her as a "forlorn" character in sweatpants. The *New York Post* used the same image under the headline "Ruth Madoff's Trashy New Life."[44]

The narrative formula—the Madoffs had A, B, and lived C, but now had X, Y, and lived Z—found wide replication. It was the formula of the fall, the formula for schadenfreude. Dramatic, almost farcical examples were found in all coverage. The *Guardian*, for instance, reported, "The disgraced Wall Street fund manager swapped a cocaine-fueled life of luxury for a prison regime in which he eats pizza cooked by a child molester and shares a prison cell with a 21-year-old drug offender."[45] The *New York Post* echoed: "He will have to tweak his taste for prime rib and cognac amid conditions that are decidedly less refined . . . Prisoner No. 61727-054 . . . munched on a microwaved meal of frozen chicken patties and canned string beans delivered to his cell in a Styrofoam container."[46] Tom Zambito of the *Daily News* wrote: "It's bye-bye forever for the $35,000 Lavar Kerman Persian carpet and the $20,000 Chippendale-style tea table . . . Home now is a Spartan cell in a maximum-security wing of lower Manhattan's Metropolitan Correctional Center, with a bunk bed and seatless metal toilet."[47]

Many of my interviewees from across the tabloid/elite and UK/US divides spoke in comparable terms of the way the story of the Madoffs' fall had emotional resonance for their readership in a time of crisis and the beginning of recession. For those who wrote for the tabloids, there was a sense that their audience felt pleasure most keenly because of their class position vis-à-vis those represented by the Madoffs. James Doran noted:

> There were all these good, honest, working people reading the *New York Post* on the subway, going to work nine hours a day for whatever they're making, aspiring to be wealthy, aspiring to be successful . . . and to see the rug pulled from under [the Madoffs] and to have them exposed as common criminals is incredibly gratifying when you're on the subway at 7 a.m. every day.

Tom Zambito of the *Daily News* also spoke to me of the emotive effect the Madoff case would have on his readers due to the class dynamics and simmering discontent with the status quo:

> The catchphrase here is "Park Avenue" . . . That's a very loaded phrase. People don't think they can make money like Bernard Madoff, but when you're at the top, people like to see you fall. It's not just Madoff; once you hit Park Avenue, that's an emblem of wealth and prosperity and privilege and all that goes along with it. It's "See what happened to him when he reached for the stars; they're all greedy!" I think people take comfort in that in some sadistic realm.

Tom Leonard, US correspondent for the UK *Telegraph*, commented, "I think greedy people who get their comeuppance is always a popular line . . . [and] here are these gullible idiots in expensive golf clubs [who were] drawn in because of their own greed." It was not only journalists writing for a primarily working- and lower-middle-class audience, though, who noted the class resentment and "sadistic" pleasure that came from watching a billionaire downgrade from Park Avenue to Metropolitan Correctional. James Bone of the London *Times*, writing for a more affluent readership, remarked in our interview:

> I think in a lot of the coverage there was the schadenfreude of revenge . . . It is emotionally satisfying for readers, *and it does suggest that in the end it's alright after all because the bad guy gets his comeuppance and has to go live in a cell with serial killers* . . . And that's not just the Madoff case, it's all the high-profile crime by rich people that the nonrich enjoy; the fall to the floor from grace and the idea that they're going to be physically suffering as a result of their high life.

Bone's statement raises an important point about the outcome of the anger and class resentment that the Madoff case produced. If, as he suggests, all is symbolically resolved through the downfall of Madoff, or if everything is "alright after all"—in other words, if we conclude that there is "justice for all" because Madoff is spending life in prison (not on a yacht)—we have made a terrible mistake. As we have seen, the financial crisis and the Madoff scandal became intertwined in reportage and intermixed in public consciousness. Moreover, the Madoff case (once it was conflated with the crisis) could be used to encapsulate all of the issues that led to the crisis and to provide the story with a clear "bad guys never win" ending by sending him and him alone to federal prison. The alternative would have been to confront the daunting totality of structural issues that could create a Madoff or a financial crisis. If we as a society were to attempt to resolve these structural issues, we might quickly find that the foundations of our economic order were resting upon a perilous precipice of debt, cronyism, corruption, and inequality.

Blaming the Victim and Greed

The anger which surfaced in response to Bernie Madoff's billion-dollar Ponzi stimulated more than a sense of schadenfreude or class resentment. Unlike in boom times, with their lower rates of unemployment, higher rates of profit, and concealment of frauds due to liquidity in the market, times of bust allow for more full-throated critique of greed. "It is already clear that the [Madoff] scandal's broader effect will be to tarnish a global financial services industry reeling from the effects of its own greed and hubris with evidence of staggering gullibility and neglect as well," the London *Times* declared.[48] The Madoff case's symbolic enmeshment with the financial crisis brought about an intense examination of the role of greed in capitalist economies broadly, the type of greed that had led to the crisis and recession but was ideologically extolled by fictitious characters like Gordon Gecko and by real-world rightest thinkers such as Ayn Rand (who notably influenced future Fed chair Alan Greenspan as teacher, confidant, and mentor). A key part of this examination focused on the alleged complicity of "greedy" victims in the perpetuation of the Madoff fraud. Class issues again surfaced in the discourse as victims were presented as belonging to dichotomous groups: those greedy, wealthy victims who "should have known better" and who became the targets of a strong blame-the-victim narrative, and those "truly innocent," guileless victims who were from modest, middle-class or working-class backgrounds and deserving of empathy.

Strong examples of the broad critiques of greed were found in several tabloid papers in the United States and United Kingdom, like *Daily*

News reporter Mike Lupica's article "Unbridled Greed Chips Away at Last Remnants of the American Dream."[49] Here Lupica gave voice to a street vendor and former veteran, "Don." Although there was no particular reason to think of Don as an expert or an everyman, Lupica portrayed him as such. Don made strong populist statements about greed in the American economy, statements that would have been unimaginable, or poorly received, during a period of boom. As the piece captures so much of the tenor of the discourse, it deserves citation:

> "You can't be surprised by greed in a country of greed," [Don said] . . . "We pay the check . . . for systemic greed that flourished under the outgoing President [George W. Bush] and his men . . . [This country] has lost its way . . . Greed has gone unregulated through one presidential administration after another, all the way back to the boom years of the sainted Ronald Reagan. But when the bottom fell out of the mortgage business and all these banks, we were told again and again that this was all the fault of poor people who overextended themselves to buy houses they could not afford; that somehow the poor sunk the economy and all these huge companies by themselves. But these things never happen in a vacuum, not with bums like Madoff, allowed to run wild in a world of money without nearly enough transparency or regulation, until it is too late."

Through "Don," the *Daily News*'s Lupica evinces the way "Madoff" became shorthand for the ethos of greed that led to the crisis of 2008, an ethos which was incubated in the neoliberal era. Anger is expressed, but also a sense of hopeless pessimism. The United States has "lost its way," and the American Dream is revealed as a false promise held out to the masses and then denied to them.

The two British tabloids analyzed for this project offered critiques of systemic greed as well, extrapolating from the greed witnessed in the Madoff case. The *Daily Mirror* claimed: "The shamed financier and his terrifyingly simple racket epitomize the amoral greed that has ruled for too long. We are all paying for their determination to get rich at any cost, which brought the economy crashing down around us."[50] In a separate article the *Mirror* would write about Madoff, "He was driven by greed, exactly the sort of avarice that brought banks to the brink of collapse across the Western world."[51] The more right-leaning *Sun* likewise posited, "In 20 years Bernie Madoff will be a byword for how thirsty for cash we were before the credit crunch."[52]

The more elite/broadsheet newspapers in America and Britain predictably did not present the same type of populist undertones found in the *Daily News*'s "Unbridled Greed Chips Away at Last Remnants of the American Dream," nor suggest as overtly as the *Daily Mirror* that greed itself had brought down world economies. Still, they did note the symbolic function the Madoff case had in epitomizing greed, and drew parallels between his greed and the criminality and misbehaviors found in other institutions entrusted with the public good. An op-ed piece in the *Washington Post* (reporting on events in the United Kingdom), for example, extended the critique of greed stirred through the Madoff case to the members of the British Parliament who were being charged with embezzlement of taxpayer funds—spending them on frivolities. "That feeling, so palpable in London—and in New York, and in Washington— that 'I'm clever, I work hard, so I deserve to be richer, even at someone else's expense' helped bring down Lehman Brothers, helped create the Madoff pyramid and has now damaged the ancient House of Commons. Which venerable institution is going to fall next?"[53]

Even Madoff indirectly implicated greed in his own crime. In prison, Bernie Madoff would several times rhetorically raise the question of why he committed his crime, and while masterfully avoiding declarative statements about his own personal greed, couched the crime as part of a broader malaise in the financial sector involving greed. "The question that now has to be answered is why and how did this happen, not only to me but to Wall Street in general," he wrote, referring to what he termed a "terribly corrupt and dangerous culture" where illegal behavior and schemes like insider trading and front running run rampant. With the caveat, "I am not holding this culture solely responsible for my own behavior, and there are many people on Wall Street that are honest and follow the rules," he went on:

> To begin to understand why all this corruption and wrongdoing, you have to start with the reality that the financial services industry is the most regulated industry in the world . . . The more regulation there is to comply with, the more

violations there are to violate. Then there is the GREED factor of making money. Both the greed of the investors and the firms and their employees. The often forgotten fact of life in investing in the market is that for every winner there is a loser—a zero sum game. The person who buys a stock believes it is going to appreciate, and the person selling the same stock to him is of the belief that it is going lower. The buyer often feels he possesses information that he alone possesses or realizes.

For the moment, I will leave aside Madoff's circular logic about regulations driving up rates of violation (which is effectively exculpatory of wrongdoing since it implies that if we want less wrongdoing we should merely eliminate some rules) and turn to his other remarks. Madoff's comments on pervasive greed—that is, the greed that is characteristic of a market economy or in the culture of Wall Street—did not, aside from distancing himself from claims of being personally infected by this greed, significantly differ from that found in the media discourses. However, some of the harshest charges of greediness were reserved for neither Wall Street speculators nor elected officials but instead for wealthy victims of Madoff's own Ponzi.

Blame the (Wealthy) Victims

A complicated series of narratives emerged and evolved over time about the Madoff victims, as they were discursively put into typologies according to their class status; the supposed likelihood of greed was seen as a motivator for their investment with him. When the story first broke, a pervasive perception would linger that most if not all of Madoff's investors were extremely wealthy, sophisticated people who were both capable and culpable. They were, in this narrative, capable of making savvy financial choices; they were therefore culpable—at the least—of turning a blind eye to their suspicions or not doing their due diligence.[54] "Caveat emptor" and the maxim "If it's too good to be true, it probably is" were widely invoked, the latter even becoming the title for Erin Arvedlund's book on the case: *Too Good to Be True: The Rise and Fall of Bernie Madoff.* John Nester, spokesperson for the SEC, expressed at the end of our interview:

I think overall the main takeout point is that no matter what, nothing changes the fundamental laws of nature when it comes to investing. The greater the risk, the greater the return. So in other words, when someone has . . . greater than normal returns, everyone should wonder how that is possible, and not rely on someone else to catch it for you.

A strong "blame the victim" narrative remained in the discourse and challenged the very notion that these investors were victims at all (except for being victimized by their own cupidity).[55] Importantly, this narrative of victim culpability assumed a moral, didactic tone similar to that found in rape cases where the victim is blamed for enticing the rapist. The investors, in this sense, had it coming to them; they were responsible; they should have known better. This was a narrative through which guilt and blame for the financial crisis could also be assigned, deflecting attention away from more structural, systemic issues within global capitalism.

The story of working- and middle-class victims surfaced more gradually, and in the United States did so primarily through tabloid reportage on individual victims, those "ordinary Joes/Janes" who had, say, lost their money through pension funds that had money with Madoff. This group of victims had their stories presented sympathetically, because they *couldn't* have known better. They were victims twice over—of Madoff yet also of those institutions and individuals who were entrusted with protecting their money but who themselves had deliberately ignored signs of fraud.

My contention that there was a dichotomization of victims in the discourse was affirmed by Erin Arvedlund, who in addition to authoring *Too Good to Be True* was the editor of a compilation of essays from Madoff victims entitled *The Club No One Wanted to Join*. When I asked if she thought the media coverage blamed the victims, she responded:

There were two camps of victims. There were those who knew better, those like Walter Noel and Sandra Manske of [the feeder fund] Tremont and others who had a lot of access to Bernie Madoff, probably knew better, saw the warning signs . . . and then there were the little people, who came in generally as indirect investors and had no clue, and had no way of *having* a clue. I would say the first camp definitely were complicit, the second were powerless to find out and were relying on really shiftless regulators like the SEC to do the due diligence for them . . . I would say the media failed to distinguish between the two types of victims.

There was, as Arvedlund asserts, a blurring together of the two groups of victims. However, this blurring was most prominent at the outset of the coverage. Prior to Madoff's sentencing in 2009, the blame-the-victim narrative as yet had not become the blame-the-wealthy-victim narrative. Immediately after the story broke in December 2008, the victims were collectively portrayed across the tabloid/broadsheet and US/UK divides as wealthy investors, willfully blind due to greed (or at least recklessly blind), and even as invidious social climbers. The *New York Post*, for instance, ran its front-page cover with the headline "WIPED OUT: Big-bucks Losers Storm the 50b 'Fraudster' Office," presenting the victims as a homogeneous group of the rich, as "big-bucks losers"—hardly a sympathetic treatment of those who had lost money in the Ponzi scheme. The use of scare quotes around the word "fraudster" also points to the skepticism with which the victims were treated. The *New York Times* would reflect the same initial perception of the victims as "big-bucks losers": "[There was] mass public outrage over Bernard Madoff, a man who *stole primarily from the well-off.*" These well-off victims "sought [Madoff] out to casually plead with him to manage their savings so they could start reaping the steady, solid returns their *envied friends* were getting."[56] In an early January 2009 article "The Rules Madoff's Investors Ignored," the *New York Times* would correspondingly report: "As much as the steady returns were enticing, Mr. Madoff's investors *wanted to bask in the glow of being part of such an elite, select group.* They didn't ask enough questions and seemingly assumed the person who got them in had vetted him."[57] In this view, there is no insinuation—victims are not tacitly accused of turning a blind eye—instead, their desire to attain social status and solidify their class position is portrayed as a tragic flaw. The *Washington Post* would go further in a December 30 article: "Not all Madoff's investors could have been in the dark . . . Some . . . I would wager, must have calculated that they could get in, get their returns, and get out before the whole thing fell apart."[58]

This early blame-the-wealthy-victim narrative in the United States was notably repeated in the UK media as well. "The level of returns seemed too good to be true, and it was. But the sense of entitlement the wealthy have to even more wealth is just too entrenched to bother with the truth," the *Guardian*'s Gary Younge wrote on December 22, 2008.[59] "Men like Mr. Madoff target the greedy," London *Times* investment commentator Carl Mortished opined. "Alongside 'Too good to be true' is another maxim that guides you past hucksters and snake-oil merchants: *it is hard to cheat an honest man.*"[60] The none-too-subtle implication was that if it was easy for Madoff to lead investors astray, then perhaps their moral compass was broken to begin with.

Andrew Clark of the London *Times* bolstered the findings of the media analysis in his description of the initial public reaction to the Madoff victims:

> I think there was quickly a perception that the victims were wealthy people themselves, that they were rich people just trying to get richer and therefore they didn't deserve sympathy in quite the same way as, say, people who had lost their homes to foreclosure or to Wall Street excess at the time . . . It was a perception that those involved were *almost universally wealthy*.

Several of the British journalists concurred, but added that they felt the narrative of greedy individual investors was particularly appealing for a UK audience because it accorded with deeply held stereotypes of Americans. James Doran, who wrote for the London *Times* as well as the *Guardian* and *New York Post*, had the unique position of being able to talk about the portrayals of victims for separate national audiences:

> When I was writing for the *Times* or for the *Guardian*, I was writing a lurid tale of greed that happened in America, where everybody is greedy and everybody's lurid . . . [With the] British reporting, you sort of augment certain stereotypes . . . It's a foreign story you're writing, you're telling people what it's like here in America. And what it's like here is there are these greedy fat cats who stole old ladies' money and that's typical of those greedy Americans. Obviously, that wasn't my point of view.

The perception of victims as universally wealthy, greedy, and accountable did not hold up throughout the reportage, however. A clear division between the two victim camps became evident in the reportage after two important events. First, Madoff's March 12, 2009, guilty plea, and then his June 16, 2009, sentencing. These events provided a forum for a breadth of victims' stories to be heard by journalists, and the stories clearly made an impact on the nature of subsequent reporting, and consequently on public views of the victims. Stephen Foley, then associate business editor at the *Independent*, provided testimony to the change in discourse:

> I started out with the view about the victims not necessarily being the most sympathetic characters . . . because his victims tended to be well-off compared to all the other people suffering economically. *I didn't really focus very much on the personal, individual stories until I sat in court at the sentencing*, where one by one these people walked up to the podium and told their story to the judge and described how their personal circumstances had changed, how their dreams had gone, and the financial worries about paying for their health and paying for their old age. You know, real stories. It was a particularly powerful moment.

There was not only a noticeable increase in the measure of sympathy allotted to the victims as a group, even those who may have started off from a position of affluence, but also an acknowledgment that middle- and working-class people had been affected deeply. The *Daily News* would report the words of victim Miriam Siegman: "There's this notion that all Madoff's victims were well-to-do, but that's not true . . . There were firefighters, teachers, garbage men and many others."[61] The *Daily Mirror*, as if to make the victims more deserving of empathy because of their class status, declared: "[They] were not just the rich and famous. He stole the savings of pensioners and funds from charities."[62]

Pathos-filled, personal descriptions of working- and middle-class victims abounded in the wake of the June sentencing. The *Daily News* included accounts such as, "Many of the emotion-racked missives to Judge Denny Chin come from elderly retirees who describe losing their life savings or being forced to reenter the workforce so they can pay for food or keep the electricity turned on";[63] or, "Carla Hirschhorn . . . says she and her husband, Stanley, lost the money they'd saved to send their daughter to college. Her mother has been forced to live on a Social Security check."[64] The *New York Post* correspondingly appealed to its readership with stories like that of a retired New York textile distributor: "'We had considered Madoff Securities not as a get-rich-quick scheme but as a buffer against risk . . . Now everything that I worked for over a 50-year career is gone.' The Brooklyn native said he'd just cashed his life-insurance policy to pay his mortgage, but was still nervous that he might lose his home."[65] Noteworthy about these *Daily News* and *Post* articles and others of their ilk is their emphasis on the hard work that the middle-class and working-class victims had engaged in prior to their involvement in the scheme. They were therefore "deserving" of sympathy from a readership also composed ostensibly of nose-to-the-grindstone working-class and middle-class readers angry about greed and social inequality evinced through the Madoff case, but also through the crisis. They could have been in a Horatio Alger story, characters who had abided by all the "rules" in order to attain their small piece of the American Dream, until a wealthy fraudster had taken that all away, while other elites had turned a blind eye. John Marzulli of the *Daily News* points out:

> In the Madoff case I would say there was some willful ignorance. Some of the victims were extremely sophisticated people, people even in the financial world. That's a different situation from somebody who works for the city who's trying to put away a nest egg for their kid's college and doesn't know anything about finance. It's hard to be willfully ignorant when you really don't understand securities or the market.

Diana Henriques of the *New York Times* likewise expressed sympathy for the less sophisticated investors, while pointing out that in fact the "If it's too good to be true" adage was not applicable to some in the fraud because Madoff's returns—between 10 and 15 percent—were not unimaginable:

> Madoff didn't even outperform the Magellan Fund. Nothing he was offering people was too good to be true, except the consistency of it, which is only visible in hindsight . . . [Some of the victims] were the retirees of the Los Angeles Bus

Drivers Union. I spoke to one; they could not tell you what the typical mutual fund was returning that year. So they didn't know whether this was an unusual return or not. Should they have known? Maybe, but we do not require financial literacy as a condition of getting a high school diploma in the United States . . . I'm sympathetic to that. For the least sophisticated victims it's very hard to argue that they should have known better. And modern commerce is impossible if nobody trusts anybody else.

The UK broadsheets' coverage also evolved over the months following Madoff's arrest, emphasizing class differences and surfacing resentments. The *Times* would write: "In addition to stealing from retirees, veterans and widows, Bernard Madoff stole from the disabled . . . Every time he cashed a cheque to spend for his family's lavish lifestyle, he killed dreams."[66] The *Guardian* quoted Adriane Biondo, whose family, including elderly relatives, had lost savings to Madoff: "This is not just a plight of the rich . . . Middle class people have lost a lot of money too."[67] The *Guardian*, in an almost self-reflexive manner, presented the testimony of a Staten Island, New York, man, Angelo Viola, seventy-nine, who wanted to distance himself from the generalized image of the victim in the media: "I live in a modest two-bedroom house and I own one car. I was a small business owner and I worked six days a week for most of my life . . . Now I am considered under poverty level and I do not think I can last another six months in my home."[68] Again, in the British coverage there is a selective narration of stories that have a strong emphasis on the hard work and sacrifice of the middle- and working-class victims to attain what they had lost in the Ponzi. They were discursively marked as more worthy of sympathy and emblematic of the postcrisis suffering of those who had nothing to do with engineering the crisis, had not been part of the elite that played Russian roulette with the economy.

Yet in spite of coverage that became more attuned to class differences, there remained even after Madoff's March 2009 plea and June 2009 sentencing a didactic, chiding vein in the discourse, particularly in the broadsheet US newspapers, and an attitude among many of my journalist interviewees that, after all, the victims should have asked more questions, should have known better. "It's up to the rest of us . . . to be a bit more wary and a little less greedy, to listen to the voices of buy-and-hold stability and to ignore the siren songs of churn, churn, churn, and Too Good to Be True," the *New York Times*'s Josh Schwartz warned.[69] In his opinion piece "Madoff Had His Accomplices: His Victims" following Madoff's guilty plea in March, Joe Nocera would describe Sharon Lissauer: "She had not been wealthy, she said, but she's lost everything . . . It was hard not to feel sad for her—indeed for all the victims of Mr. Madoff's evil doing. *But one also has to wonder, what were they thinking?* I suppose you could argue that most of Mr. Madoff's direct investors lacked the ability or the financial sophistication . . . But it shouldn't have mattered."[70]

Even after the marathon of hearing 113 victim-impact statements at Madoff's sentencing,[71] the *Guardian* noted, "It has been difficult to drum up much public sympathy for [the victims] since a lot of them were rich and, one presumes, a little bit greedy."[72] Ed Pilkington of the *Guardian* spoke to me in the paper's Soho office of a less-than-wholehearted sympathy:

> Often it was Florida Jewish retirees whose pensions were lost, often could no longer help their kids buy a place, and so it was fairly wrenching stuff. I can remember feeling sympathy, and I think the papers were probably very sympathetic to those people who lost everything. But I think there was probably another strain, . . . maybe a little bit of coldness towards victims on one level because these are very rich people.

Anton Antonowicz of the *Daily Mirror* joked:

> There's an awful lot of greedy people out there—just as much as there's an awful lot of needy people out there. Certainly I think many of his victims were the greedy needy! [*laughter*]. I felt sorry for some of them, if I took my journalistic hat off. But to be perfectly honest, not *hugely* sorry. I mean—*buyer beware!* They bought into Madoff.

The legitimacy of these attitudes, however, especially as they apply to the middle- and working-class victims of Madoff, is questionable given the manner in which they became embroiled in the Ponzi. As Diana Henriques wrote in *Wizard of Lies*, "As with everyone who stayed at this party until the bitter end, it comes down to separating the villains from the victims, the knaves from the fools."[73] No easy task. The Madoff Victim Fund (the Department of Justice Asset Forfeiture Distribution Program) received 63,737 claims in 135 countries from direct and indirect investors in Madoff.[74] It is true that many did personally "buy into Madoff" and actually withdrew more from BLMIS than they had deposited over the years, thus earning the designation of "net winners."[75] There were clients like Jeffry Picower, a New York investor who would withdraw $5.1 billion in "profit," that is, fraudulent returns, over twenty years from several Madoff accounts, including an account that in 1999 earned an outrageous 950 percent return;[76] or Carl Shapiro, a Palm Beach entrepreneur and philanthropist who had invested in Madoff for decades, who withdrew hundreds of millions in fictitious profits.[77] There were also the heads of the Madoff "feeder funds" like Stanley Chais, who "earned" over $200 million in fees for, often unknowingly, steering investors into the Madoff fund,[78] and who withdrew hundreds of millions more from the funds in "profits." Madoff, referring to these investors, would present himself too as a victim of their greed. "Believe me," he would write,

> everyone used me in one form or another, including my investors. Remember that many of my clients date back to the 1960's and made legitimate profits averaging in the teens or better. The claw back [lawsuits] were limited to the last 6 years of my business. Do you have any idea how much money they earned and kept?[79]

While the Picowers and Shapiros are extreme examples, the GAO's "Report on Customer Outcomes in the Madoff Liquidation Proceedings" revealed that "for individuals, the total net investment position at the time of the Madoff firm's failure was 767 million, meaning they [were net winners and] had withdrawn more money than they had initially invested"; these were 60 percent of individual investors. Sociologist Jock Young, arguably one of the most important criminologists of the late twentieth and early twenty-first centuries, would critically note: "It has to be remembered that it was the cupidity of Madoff's clients that was the real motor behind the scheme, and that it was they who benefited year in and year out until the final collapse . . . Once Madoff was arrested, his greedy Palm Beach investors considered themselves, with breathtaking hypocrisy, victims."

However, 25 percent of Madoff account holders were institutional accounts such as pension funds and charities, and these were on average "net losers"—they had deposited three billion dollars more than they had withdrawn. Included in this category were those "everyday" cops and firefighters whose pensions were tied to Madoff or who had thought they were placing their retirement funds in a diversified fund. Jock Young would, with reservation, admit in reference to these individuals, "There were relatively poor victims who deserve our concern, but they played more of a role in the rhetoric of victimization than they did in the proportion of losses." To add to the plight of these victims, the Madoff trustee, Irving Picard, "determined [that] under SIPA only those who had invested directly with the Madoff firm were customers for claims purposes." Thus, working-class members of the Bricklayers and Allied Craftsmen Local 2 Annuity Fund and the International Brotherhood of Electrical Workers Local Union 43, for example, whose benefit funds were invested in Madoff feeder funds, were ineligible for recovery of those funds from Picard.[80]

Madoff from prison would go on to repeatedly invoke the greed of his wealthy investors (while professing his remorse for the scheme and proclaiming his attempts to make investors whole), their willful blindness, or even complicity. "I was subjected to the lies and cries of victims that were [at the court] to speak. All of which were anything but the desperate and homeless victims they claimed to be." But what about the small-time, unsophisticated investors like the firefighters who lost their pensions, I queried. "Those investors were brought in without my knowledge," he stated, and with a remarkable lack of appreciation of irony, added:

> The absurdity was that there were numerous partnerships formed that were not supposed to be taking in small individuals that did not meet the financial requirements to come in directly. Whenever we found out, the accounts were closed. So much for honesty.

Madoff and Inequality in the Criminal Justice System

The "tough on crime" era of mass incarceration inaugurated in the United States in the 1970s, with its harsh sentencing practices that would increase the number of people in prisons or jails by 500 percent to over two million in the 2000s, was fueled by popular, racialized fear of "superpredators,"[81] gang violence, and drugs—street crimes. Politicians stoked the coals of this panic and large segments of the media and public fed into the frenzy. Crime (but not the white-collar variety) was the number one concern of Americans by the mid-1990s.[82] Sociologist Stanley Cohen's classic theoretical term "moral panic" can be used to identify this milieu. For Cohen, a moral panic happens when a "condition, episode, person or group of persons emerges to become defined as a threat to societal values and interests; its nature is presented in stylized and stereotypical fashion; the moral barricades are manned by editors, bishops, politicians and other right-thinking people; socially accredited experts pronounce their diagnoses and solutions."[83]

In the 1990s, when street crime topped this list of Americans' concerns, constructing white-collar crime as a social problem of the same magnitude as street crime, or white-collar criminals as comparatively "dangerous" characters, would have been risible. But as sociologist Michael Jacobson identified in his *Downsizing Prisons: How to Reduce Crime and End Mass Incarceration*, by the early 2000s, as more Americans recognized the decline in crime, and other concerns (like terrorism after September 11) surfaced, street crime had been displaced from its centrality as a concern. When asked the same question about the most important issue in 2009, 86 percent of Americans polled said economic issues were their number one concern. With the displacement of street offenses as the chief bogeyman of American concerns, and economics assuming center stage, a fascinating discourse was given the space to emerge about inequalities present in the criminal justice system that aligned popular opinion with conclusions critical criminologists have long espoused. White-collar crime as a social problem, one that caused vast amounts of harm analogous to violent crime, now could be broached without one being labeled a communist or lefty, and white-collar offenders viewed as criminals. The perceived leniency toward white-collar crime in spite of its enmeshment with casino capitalism only strengthened this perspective.

In the same media outlets that had most vocally proclaimed the age of the superpredator could be found the most emphasis on class inequalities in the criminal justice system, skewing that system against the poor in favor of the rich. The US tabloids struck strong populist tones in their appeal to a more working-class audience who would presumably respond with anger. Left-leaning British tabloids like the *Daily Mirror* were also willing to approach the class inequalities manifested through the treatment of Madoff. The US "elite" papers, however (*New York Times* and *Washington Post*), dedicated very little ink to presenting this discourse. And although the UK broadsheets the *Guardian* and the *Times* offered more attention to class-based disparities, they did not have the same populist overtones found in the tabloids, the same sense of outrage.

Discourse about white-collar crime as a problem causing harm and thus equally deserving of attention as "street" offenses was exemplified in editorials like that written by Stanley Crouch of the *Daily News*. In his "Whether the Weapon Is a Pencil or Hot Lead, a Thug's Still a Thug," he declared: "We now know that it is as much about crime in the suites as crime in the streets. Our recession proves that white-collar crime is finally *the most dangerous and threatening to us all . . .* [Madoff's] counterparts on the lower rungs went at it the raw way, using violence and easily observable theft and corruption. The difference is not in the soul of the person but in the means necessary to commit the crime."[84] Crouch's assessment that white-collar crime is more dangerous and threatening than "street" crime, and its appearance in a major US tabloid, represented a significant shift in the discourse about crime, an awakening class consciousness of inequality and the ways in which attention to the crimes of the poor had been distractions. Even though the estimated cost of white-collar crime per year has exceeded that of robbery, burglary, larceny, and motor vehicle theft by billions (the estimated cost of white-collar crimes soars into the hundreds of billions in the US and the UK), the cases have been typically found in the business pages. Thus, such crimes are made to seem more innocuous and the public mind is anesthetized to their dangerous and pernicious effects.

The UK tabloid the *Daily Mirror*'s headlines "Two-tier Justice System? You Can Bank on That" and "Justice Turns a Blind Eye to the Super Rich,"[85] which referenced Madoff but also incorporated discussion of British white-collar crimes, hinted that conversations about class in criminal justice were emerging in Britain during the crisis. "Do ordinary workers still wear blue shirts? . . . Because it's clear there are different rules for men with a blue collar and the gentlemen with a white one," journalist Maurice Fitzmaurice wrote in the latter article. He compared the prison sentence of eight months given to a man for cheating on his unemployment benefits to the lack of punishment of bankers such as Anglo Irish Bank's notorious former chairman Sean Fitzpatrick. Fitzpatrick, among other transgressions, had hidden over a million euros in personal loans from Anglo Irish. Fitzmaurice proclaimed: "Justice is blind and we're all equal in the eyes of the law—or so we're told. And at that money-to-years ratio (8 months for cheating unemployment), bankers wouldn't live long enough to finish the sentence. The bigger the crime, the smaller the time." Sir Ken Macdonald, in an editorial piece for the London *Times*, quipped: "If you mug someone in the street and you are caught, chances are that you will go to prison. In recent years, mugging someone out of their savings or their pension would probably earn you a yacht."[86]

Beyond the general critiques of justice systems riddled with class bias, the media seized on specific, visible examples of such bias throughout the Madoff case. Madoff's release to his Upper East Side apartment on "bail monitoring," pending his trial, was the subject of much consternation and anger as it brought into stark relief the vastly different treatments between white-collar and "street" criminals in spite of gross disparities in the amount of harm done. Tom Leonard noted in our interview: "So many other people who are arrested for crimes go straight to prison. It seems to be another example of how the rich man can play by different rules."

Not only was Madoff allowed to stay in his home, which had already aroused class resentment through its lavishness and luxury, but the bail monitoring showcased the privileges of the elite in their ability to avoid sitting in jail by hiring a private guard—even if this wealth may have been derived from wrongdoing. The *New York Post* dubbed Madoff "the Prisoner of Park Avenue," "held captive in a palatial penthouse,"[87] while the *Daily News* sardonically wrote, "To paraphrase Mark Twain, steal a loaf of bread, go to prison, steal $50 billion, go home to your penthouse."[88] In a separate article, the *Daily News* would also note that "[Madoff] has been lounging in his $7 million penthouse while shoplifters and other petty criminals in this city are routinely held on bail beyond their means."[89] And the London *Times* reported, "Mr. Madoff . . . is under 24-hour house arrest at the Upper East Side apartment building replete with white-gloved doormen and residents who include Matt Lauer, the television personality."[90]

At one level, it seemed that the moment was ripe for transformative change out of the rubble of the financial crisis. Our attention was focused on the crime and punishment of one of the elite. Furthermore, we were able to see the ways in which wealth continued to translate into privilege within the criminal justice system. Yet looking back over the discourse, we see that there is no evidence of such creative reimagining. Jock Young's analysis in "Moral Panic: Its Origins in Resistance, Ressentiment, and Translation of Fantasy into Reality" suggests a reason why, given what we have seen through this chapter about how discourse formed around the Madoff case.

According to Young, in meritocratic, individualistic societies such as the United States and the United Kingdom, when the pursuit of the American Dream (and its European equivalent) is held up to everyone as a real possibility but in truth is denied to many through structural impediments, there are several potential reactions to this reality. The individual may be blamed—we hear this through narratives about the "undeserving" or "lazy poor," the narratives of the "loser" who doesn't use all of her opportunities to rise in life. Failures of the system and structural forces can be blamed. Or, as Young suggests, a particular class of people can be blamed, who (due in part to relative deprivation and glaring inequalities) are perceived as preventing members of other groups from achieving the Dream. If this occurs, a feeling of *ressentiment* arises. He quotes sociologist Robert Merton in describing three key elements of *ressentiment*: first, "diffuse feelings of hate, envy, and hostility; second, a sense of being powerless to express these feelings *actively* against the person or social stratum evoking them; and third, a continual re-experiencing of this impotent hostility." The schadenfreude experience of seeing Madoff, a representative of the elite class, fall; the focus on the greed of Madoff as well as that of his wealthier victims— these hostilities which surfaced in the narratives about the case ultimately were not active, but passive. They were discursive. To get beyond mere *ressentiment*, a complete change in values, a renunciation of the pursuit of a materialistic American Dream would need to occur. "*Ressentiment* involves a sour grapes pattern . . . In *ressentiment*, one condemns what one secretly craves; in rebellion, one condemns the craving itself."[91]

Because there was no rebellion, there was no change in values. There was however a condemnation through punishment (to be explored in the next chapter) and an attempt to resolve the problems with capitalism unearthed during the crisis symbolically, condemning the "craving" via Bernie Madoff and other white-collar offenders who previously had been obscured by the focus on crimes of the poor. The target may have shifted, but the individualist narrative prevailed. *Ressentiment* could continue and so could the current financial structure; instead of rebellion we would denounce the few bad apples, let the system continue on in untarnished operation, and leave the original Dream intact, in all its sordid materialism, to be held out to the masses.

5 BOIL HIM IN OIL: CRACKING DOWN ON WALL STREET THROUGH MADOFF

Because [Madoff] inflicted pain and suffering on unknowing victims in order to achieve an undeserved lavish lifestyle, every day in prison for the rest of his life he should eat nothing but tasteless Nutri-loaf and clean latrines. Then and only then will we victims come close to being satisfied.

—Robert Blecker, professor of criminal law at NYU and Madoff victim

If there could be a Charles Manson of Ponzi crimes, he was it. If there is a criminal category "the *worst*," he was the *worst*. If you want to think the worst mass murder, the worst gangster, the worst bank robber, . . . he was the worst Ponzi fraudster. Did he kill anybody? Did he cause anybody to shed blood? *No.* He wasn't a violent person but he was bad. He was *Bad* with a capital *B.*

—John Marzulli, *Daily News,* personal interview

THE CALLS FOR PUNISHMENT for Bernie Madoff by his victims and the public were ferocious. Proposed methods for executing Madoff (offered with varying degrees of seriousness) included forms largely abandoned due to their inhumaneness: the electric chair and hanging as well as biblical techniques like stoning.[1] For those who were squeamish about inflicting a death sentence, other harsh, creative punishments were offered. A former Manhattan prosecutor was quoted in the *New York Post* as saying—perhaps only partially in jest—"The whole world wants to see him in the same dungeon as (Alexander Dumas' famous fictional prisoner) the Count of Monte Cristo."[2] A *Daily News* reporter in describing the victims wrote, "These folks probably think the medieval body cage with spikes in the groin area . . . would be a more appropriate cell for Madoff."[3] Even Nobel Peace Prize winner and Holocaust survivor Elie Wiesel, bilked of millions in personal savings and whose Elie Wiesel Foundation for Humanity lost $15.2 million to Madoff, proposed: "I would like him to be in a solitary cell with a screen, and on that screen, for at least five years of his life, every day and every night there should be pictures of his victims. One after the other after the other, always saying, 'Look, look what you have done to this poor lady, look what you have done to this child.'"[4]

The prominence of such harsh discourse in the media, while it surely contained genuine expressions of retributionist outrage against Madoff's particular crime, also transcended his case. Although his crime had affected thousands of individuals and institutions and involved billions in real and fictitious profits, these were not the sole reasons for the retributionist tone. His trial became imbued with metaphoric meaning. Talking about the trial became a way of talking about punishment not only for Madoff but for those responsible for the financial crisis and those who continued to threaten the integrity of the capitalist system. Madoff became a proxy for a larger set of retributionist urges. After all, an entire economic order had been destabilized and, in the process, the vulnerability of the livelihoods of hundreds of millions had been exposed. Furthermore, this rude awakening had not occurred as the result of some natural disaster but instead was the product of the criminal conduct of the titans of finance, who were never prosecuted, nor did they face any other personal repercussions. To make the matter more astonishing and appalling, both before and after the crisis these same titans were often held up as self-reliant and exemplary in their possession of the technical and leadership skills necessary for personal survival in the new economy.

Madoff's consignment to 150 years in a federal prison (a number obtained through the summation of the statutory maximum sentence for all eleven counts faced[5]) provided a *symbolic* resolution to the collective anger in the United States and United Kingdom that—other than through complete reform or even revolution—could not be resolved. He offered a "fix" for all the other improprieties and crimes that went unpunished, including the class inequalities and greed and the feelings of *ressentiment* explored earlier. It was a kind of degradation ceremony such as that described by sociologist Harold Garfinkel, allowing for moral indignation to foster solidarity against Madoff and those he represented, showing him as "ritually separated from a place in the legitimate order . . . standing at a place opposed to it."[6]

Schadenfreude and *ressentiment* were evident in the desire expressed by several victims to see the formerly wealthy financial criminal engaged in the most menial and demeaning work possible—a man who would never have performed manual labor and in fact wrote large checks to have other people do it for him: $885 per month for a gardener and $2,860 for housekeeping. The letter by NYU professor and Madoff victim Robert Blecker to the *New York Times* offered this type of proposal for punishment: "Because he inflicted pain and suffering on unknowing victims in order to achieve an undeserved lavish lifestyle, every day in prison for the rest of his life he should eat nothing but tasteless Nutriloaf and clean latrines. Then, and only then will we victims come close to being satisfied."[7] In similar scatological fashion, another victim voiced in the *Daily News*, "I think latrine cleaning would be appropriate for a neat freak."[8] While not as graphic about specificities, a lawyer for the victims was quoted by the *New York Times* as saying Madoff "should never see the light of day, and in fact be sentenced to *hard* labor."

The conditions under which Madoff should be imprisoned reflected also an impulse for punishment that went beyond the sheer number of years he should be incarcerated, involving degradation that would contrast directly with his previous life of luxury. The London *Times*'s James Bone reported on one victim's impact statement: "He deserves no better than to live under a bridge in a cardboard box, scavenging for his food and clothing, living an existence which he has undoubtedly relegated some unfortunate victims to."[9] "I would love for him to have nothing," another victim told the *New York Times*. "Bernie should rot with the rats," uttered a friend of René-Thierry Magon de la Villehuchet, the French aristocrat who committed suicide after learning about his fund's enormous losses through Madoff.[10]

Religiosity was also a key theme interlaced in these discourses. Manichean, metaphysical terms like "Good" and "Evil," as well as numerous Judeo-Christian biblical references to sin, redemption, heaven, Satan, and hell, were employed, particularly in the US coverage, reflective of America's higher levels of religiosity. What Madoff (and those responsible for the crisis, by extrapolation) did, then, was seen not only as a transgression of criminal, "secular" law but as a taboo violation of the "sacred." Sacred trusts in the market and in the individuals charged with the preservation and growth of wealth had been broken through the profanity of the fraud, and the response correspondingly was couched in religious terms as a moral transgression incurring the full wrath of the collective. As NYU law professor Stephen Gillers explained in the *New York Times*: "*It's no longer about Bernard Madoff*, or even about concepts like retribution and deterrence. 'We're making a statement to ourselves about the kind of people we are . . . and what we will not accept.'"[11]

The frequent equation of Madoff with Judeo-Christian conceptions of evil and the Devil, and his subsequent consignment to hell, was found most in the US papers. He had been metaphorically expelled from heaven and from civil society, and his actions were presented as so terrible that he would continue to be judged for them in the afterlife; his punishment on earth would be just the beginning. House representative Peter King was quoted as calling Madoff "an evil person. It's morally disgraceful."[12] Victims often used these theological concepts to describe their wishes for his punishment. The head of a Georgia temple, Judith Schindler, was quoted in the *Daily News*: "Madoff will not only stand in the courts to be judged and sentenced, one day he will stand before God."[13] And Schindler's assertion was comparatively generous. The *Daily News* headline "Live a Long Life in Hell, Vics Say"[14] and the *New York Post*'s "Bern in Hell"[15] captured the tenor of much of the recorded sentiments, reporting on one victim who called Madoff "the devil incarnate" and argued that he spend the "rest of his days in a five-by-ten foot cell until his trip to eternal damnation." Correspondingly, the paper ran an article "The Devil in the Details" featuring a photoshopped image of Madoff with red horns emerging from his forehead.[16] When prosecutors made progress toward negotiating a plea with Madoff, the *Daily News* declared on their front-page headline that this was a "Deal with the Devil."[17]

Madoff-as-the-Devil gained increased currency in pop cultural representation during this time. Countless political cartoons featured Madoff with horns, as the Devil himself, or in conversation with the Devil.[18] Marketing opportunities were not to be missed, and a New

York City artist soon had released a limited edition "Bernie in Hell" habanero hot sauce. Text on the bottle read, "You can take the money but can you take ... the heat?!!!"[19] A "'Smash Me Bernie' Madoff Devil Doll" by Phoenix-based company Mini-Me ModelWorks also premiered at the New York City Toy Fair in 2009. The pitchfork-toting doll, dressed completely in red, also came with a golden hammer in order to, as the *New York Times* reported, "pulverize Mr. Madoff in effigy."[20] These demonic presentations of Madoff not only assisted in dehumanizing Madoff (making it easier to characterize his crime as inorganic to the economic system, and him as beyond civil society); as described in Chapter 2, characterizations of Madoff should also be questioned for their function as a type of dog whistle, speaking—perhaps at a subconscious level—to concealed patterns of anti-Semitism in Western culture. Joshua Trachtenberg, in *The Devil and the Jews*, and other scholars have shown how demonic representations of Jews have featured in European and American symbolism since medieval times. As "Lost in Translation: Anti-Semitic Stereotypes Based on Mistranslations" states: "In the Early Middle Ages, the leaders of the Church referred to verses in the New Testament that stated that Jews were direct descendants of the devil and came to associate Jews with evil . . . Art, poetry, drama, and religious instruction identified Jews with the Devil. Jews were portrayed not only with horns, but also tails . . . The propaganda that reinforced these stereotypes in the art, poetry, and drama consumed by the masses, le[d] to deeply rooted and pervasive stereotypes which still can be found today."[21]

Whether or not one concludes that anti-Semitism was an ingredient in the demonic representation of Madoff, his fraud affected disproportionately those in Jewish communities, and feelings of betrayal from that community were expressed in the desire to punish. The *New York Times*, in "For Jews, Madoff Scandal Brings Feelings of Betrayal and Shame," would quote Rabbi Burtron Visotzky of the Jewish Theological Seminary: "The fact that he stole from Jewish charities puts him in a special circle of hell."[22] In an editorial also for the *Washington Post*, Richard Cohen would invoke the distinguished medieval Torah scholar Maimonides:

"To fully comprehend Bernie's evil you have to know something about Maimonides . . . He codified the solemn obligation to be charitable . . . Bernie took the money intended for charity . . . This is evil." Although written from the standpoint of pre-Renaissance Catholicism, Dante's *Inferno* became a favored literary allusion, as the nature and scale of Madoff's betrayal made the connection apt and also tapped into deeply resonant cultural symbols. The London *Times Magazine* would go so far as to label the case a "modern morality tale."[23] Indeed, in "If Bernie Met Dante," Ralph Blumenthal of the *New York Times* mused: "If even that [150-year] dose of clinical justice seems like paltry penance . . . the [victims] can always turn to literature for a further measure of satisfaction . . . It is easy to imagine where [Dante] would consign this scam artist . . . to the Pit, the Ninth (and deepest) Circle of Hell. It is where sins of betrayal are punished in a sea of ice fanned frigid by the six batlike wings of the immense, three-faced, fanged and weeping Lucifer . . . poetic justice indeed."[24]

The connections made between the Madoff fraud and Judeo-Christian theology as well as a medieval morality tale were not limited to discourse found within the media. The actual sentencing of Madoff to 150 years by Judge Denny Chin became an intensely symbolic performance of punishment intended to metaphorically expel evil, to restore and give faith again to a system that had been threatened by Madoff's actions and, by extension, the actions of all who had not been arrested for wrongdoing during the crisis. Judge Chin's statement during Madoff's sentencing on June 29, 2009, was thus couched in this language of good, evil, and morality. As reported in the *Daily News*, Chin declared, "Here the message must be sent that Mr. Madoff's crimes were *extraordinarily evil* and that this kind of manipulation of the system is not just a bloodless crime that takes place on paper, but one instead that takes a staggering toll."[25] The phrase "extraordinarily evil" rang out ubiquitously across the coverage in America and Britain, more than any other phrase uttered by Chin. *Washington Post* journalist Tomoeh Murakami Tse, who was present in the court during Madoff's sentencing, reflected on Chin's choice of language:

I think it's unusual for a federal judge to use that term [*evil*] because it's not a legal term. I don't think Judge Chin is known for using those kinds of phrases lightly. He said he received a lot of mail from victims; he read one of them particularly touching from a woman that was heart-wrenching . . . He gave [Madoff] the maximum sentence, which is also unusual.

Andrew Clark, who writes for the London *Times*, reacted more strongly against the religious connotations and references in Chin's sentencing and statements, perhaps reflecting the social reality that religion occupies a much more prominent space in American life and politics:

I don't like the idea of any judge using the world "evil." "Right" and "wrong" are entirely adequate. "Good" and "evil"—that is probably an area which we should leave to the priests.

Receiving less reportage than his phrase "extraordinarily evil" but still significant and illustrative of the way Madoff's trial was transformed into a morality tale to bulwark capitalism, Judge Chin also declared during the sentencing: "In a society governed by rule of law, Mr. Madoff will get what he deserves and will be punished by his *moral culpability* . . . Trust was broken in a way that has left many—victims as well as many others—*doubting our financial institutions, our financial systems, our government's ability to regulate and protect*."

These words are crucial. The *moral* culpability for which Madoff would receive his 150-year sentence was directly tied to the smooth, taken-for-granted continuance of capitalism, which had already been deep in crisis *before* the Madoff scam had emerged. Madoff is made responsible for raising doubt in these systems, and his incarceration was about restoring confidence in the financial system. The use of morality and religion gave the full weight of collective anger to the ruling, his fraud turned to heresy.

A dearth of alternative, less punitive narratives and sensibilities, especially among the US journalists reporting on the Madoff story, revealed just how much the case had served to unify public opinion during a time of uncertainty. It provided a "quick fix" and a source of unity and cohesion. Erin Arvedlund of *Barron's* and editor of the compilation of victim/survivor essays *The Club No One Wanted to Join* described both her reaction and that of the victims who contributed to the book:

> How do you go about punishing a financial serial killer? I think whatever you can dream up would be fitting . . . Most of those [victims] expressed the sentiment that the punishment sent a message. And Judge Denny Chin did want to send a message. They wanted something a little more . . . —what's the right word, *penitence*—they wanted Bernie Madoff to have to sit in his cell and watch video of the victims over and over.

As with Chin's sentence, Arvedlund's choice of words here about the victims' wishes ties the secular with the sacred—penitence carrying with it religious connotations.

Gary Silverman of the *Financial Times* compared Madoff's sentence to those imprisoned for street crimes, such as theft, while expressing his general support for the sentence, thus continuing also the theme of increased awareness of social inequality:

> People do five, six years for stealing a hundred dollars. He stole an amazing amount of money. My father was a police reporter for many years; I grew up around a lot of such stories and the old line is, "Don't do the crime if you can't do the time."

Many of my other US interviewees felt the 150-year sentence was widely approved of by the general public and symbolically important during the crisis. And they themselves did not comment pejoratively about the sentence. Kaja Whitehouse of the *New York Post* recalled the general reaction to the news through a personal anecdote:

> I remember visiting my brother and his wife in Virginia. And she never reads the news, and even she knew who Bernie Madoff was and she said . . . *Wow!* I feel like everybody cheered at that moment, they were very happy, it was a feeling of redemption and justice.

Leslie Wayne of the *New York Times* and Ed Pilkington of the *Guardian* likewise concurred with Whitehouse that the general sentiment in the United States was one of collective elation. Wayne commented:

I don't think there was a lot of sympathy out there for Madoff . . . Even if people were asleep at the switch, you still had to look at who was the perpetrator of the crime. Who was the one who invented it? And what has the impact been on peoples' lives? So I don't think anyone is shedding a tear for the sentence he got.

Pilkington, who has also reported extensively about capital punishment in the United States, concurred: "I'm sure there are thousands of people who felt, 'Execute him, it'll be better than keeping him alive in prison.' Such is retribution in the American penal system."

Several journalists, including the *Washington Post*'s Zachary Goldfarb and the London *Times*'s Alexandra Frean, in vocalizing their support of the sentence focused on Judge Chin's contention that Madoff's crime was not a "bloodless one," suggesting that the boundaries between "street" and "white collar" crime were beginning to become murkier in the realm of public discourse, and the word "violence" contested as the grounds for distinguishing between the two types of crime. As Goldfarb said:

One hundred and fifty years was meant to be symbolic, obviously . . . It was just the court saying that significant cases of white-collar crime where you cause massive destruction and devastation to peoples' lives should be treated in a way that's not white-collar crime, [but] that's *violent* crime . . . This is basically a violent act against peoples' livelihood.

Frean, echoing Goldfarb, acknowledged that she felt Madoff should spend the rest of his life in prison. The fraud was more than "paper" losses, with potentially fatal consequences:

Even if you take the suicides of René-Thierry Magon de la Villehuchet, William Foxton, and Mark Madoff out of it, you can't say he didn't kill anyone . . . Bad things happen as a result of not having any money. You just don't know—I think that's the trouble with financial crime, particularly when the victims are older people. You can't say it didn't kill them. He showed total disregard for that. He never sat down and thought about the suffering he was causing, but somewhere in his brain he must have been aware. If you take someone's lifesavings, and they're elderly and that's all they've got, you're reducing their ability to look after themselves. So I think his crime is enormous.

Complementing the narrative of justified harsh punishment for Madoff was a strong populist sensibility found in the UK tabloid papers the *Daily Mirror* and the *Sun* (as well as in the broadsheet the London *Times*, but in more limited fashion), which held that the model of justice evinced in the United States through the Madoff trial was an exemplary one that should be replicated in Britain. Through the Madoff case the United States was presented as being tough on financial criminals (a quality allegedly lacking in the UK) and by extension more willing to prosecute those responsible for the crisis than their British counterparts. The right-leaning *Sun* went so far as to applaud the Madoff decision, comparing the justice he received with what he would have presumably received in Britain: "Well done to the US District Judge Denny Chin, who gave fraudster Bernie Madoff 150 years in jail for his £38 billion crime. Any chance of bringing him over here to set new tariffs for UK criminals?"[26] A letter to the editor of the *Sun* from a Glasgow-based writer expressed and extended the same sentiment: "May I take this opportunity to congratulate the American criminal justice system for giving a corrupt director, Bernard Madoff, a 150-year jail sentence. We should follow suit by jailing the corrupt politicians who run this country!"[27] Another opinion piece would continue: "In Britain, the criminal gets away with murder. In America, they punish them severely. *Just look at Madoff.* He got 150 years. Over here, he would have been lucky to have got 15 to 20."[28]

The left-leaning *Daily Mirror* promulgated the same narrative as its right-leaning counterpart, often using the 150-year sentence rendered in the Madoff case to point out the lack of prosecution for those responsible for the collapse of Anglo Irish Bank, especially Sean Fitzpatrick, its former chairman. An op-ed, "Untouchable Bankers Still Living It Up," declared: "The way Ireland and the US have dealt with those responsible for the financial meltdown couldn't be more different. The US government set up a special task force to hunt down bankers whose reckless behavior nearly destroyed the entire financial system . . . Bernie Madoff, the King of Wall Street as he was dubbed, was sentenced to 150 years in jail within a couple of months. Contrast this with how the Irish

Government has tackled its biggest ever financial mess."[29] In a separate editorial, Pat Flanagan for the *Daily Mirror* queried, "Why, when the likes of US corporate fraudster Bernie Madoff is serving 150 years in a North Carolina prison, has not a single file on the gangsters who destroyed our economy been sent to the D[irector of Public Prosecutions]?"[30] Note again in these narratives a strong conflation of Madoff and the white-collar wrongdoers who precipitated the financial crisis. Note also the mistaken implication that because the US government was bringing down this fraudster in such spectacular fashion, it would go on to zealously prosecute other white-collar crimes and criminals.

In more limited fashion, the broadsheet UK publications also seized on the Madoff ruling as somehow emblematic of how financial criminals were being punished in the United States in general, and went on to present the United States as a model to emulate. The London *Times*, for instance, ran the op-ed "The Wages of Sin: Madoff's Life Sentence Should Galvanize Regulators Everywhere, Including Britain," stating: "The US may boast some of the most spectacular frauds, but also the most public convictions. The 'perp walk'—the intentional march of the perpetrator of white-collar crime, stripped of his swanky suit and chauffeur-driven limo and dressed in an orange jump suit and bundled into the back of a squad car—serves a valuable purpose *in a free-market economy* to show everyone that no one is above the law. By comparison, Britain's record in tackling financial crime is appalling. Madoff's exemplary sentence will, at the least, send a warning to financiers across America. The lesson should be heeded here too."[31] The inclusion of the phrase "in a free-market economy" here is telling, as it reiterates the threat to the free market caused by those like Madoff, who would shake trust in its ineluctability. The title of the piece, "The Wages of Sin," also suggests the transmutation of Madoff's crime to the realm of the religious.

The lack of critique of Madoff's sentence, in fact its overall laudation by the British press—especially in the tabloids—is unusual. The United States is known for its exceptionalism but not usually admired for its harsh and retributive justice system in comparison to Europe. For instance, the retention of capital punishment in the United States for decades after its abolition in the United Kingdom has drawn much criticism and is the subject of extensive scholarship by sociologists like David Garland and Frank Zimring.[32] The European Union's policy on the death penalty unequivocally states, "The [EU] holds a strong and principled position against the death penalty; its abolition is a key objective for the Union's human rights policy."[33] Whereas in Europe "mainstream middle-class sentiment . . . now regards the death penalty as being ethically tainted as the crimes that produced the sentence,"[34] in America death-penalty support remains, as of 2015, a majority-supported opinion.[35] Other harsh justice policies, such as life without parole sentencing, which is given to one in thirty-five prisoners in the United States, have been abolished in five European nations. And although Britain does use life without parole for "exceptionally serious" cases, it is with a frequency dwarfed by the United States.[36]

Despite differing views on the death penalty and in spite of other indications of a cultural sensibility that would reject harsh sentencing, almost none of the British journalists interviewed about their work on the Madoff case questioned the severity of sentencing. In fact, only Andrew Clark of the London *Times* departed entirely from the narrative of punitiveness that pervaded the coverage. In his response, he raised philosophical questions about the nature of the harm done as well as concerns about the humaneness of the sentence:

> I thought it was an idiotic sentence, to be honest. One hundred and fifty years is clearly very silly. First of all, the issue of lining his crime up against violent crimes—he wasn't found killing people. Yet he was put in prison for longer than most murderers get on. Secondly, the issue of being merciful to someone at the end of their lives. Fifteen years would have been entirely adequate. You still would have the hope of getting out and having the last few years of freedom. It reminds me a little bit of when the Lockerbie bomber was released by the Scottish government on the grounds he should be allowed to die with his family. That would have done incredibly bad in America, where there doesn't seem really to be any kind of exception for being merciful.

Tom Leonard of the *Daily Telegraph*, while he had a similar incredulous reaction to the sentence's length—saying, "I personally find, possibly other media people do in Britain as well, that these kind of bizarre

American 500,000 years in prison to be rather ridiculous"—did not voice the same qualms as Clark. However, he rationalized the sentence and support for it in both the United States and the United Kingdom as a sign of the times:

> I think many people felt Madoff deserved to go away; that's another result of the economic crisis, . . . the anti–Wall Street pity feeling. It's the same in Britain to a certain extent with an anti-city and anti-London attitude that [says] white-collar crime is as serious as a lot of other crimes, and that people who commit them deserve to go to prison. I think for Madoff, he was going away to prison for the rest of his life. Whether it's thirty years or one hundred and fifty years, it still comes down to the same thing.

Leonard's comments suggest that the nature of the transgression as a financial crime during a time of crisis prevented any "pity" from emerging, but also made the point that Madoff's age (71 at the time) rendered the "actual" 150 years to be the equivalent of, say, 15 or 20 years and therefore precluded criticism of harsh punishment. Several of my interviews with other British journalists corroborated the latter explanation offered by Leonard. They would remark that the number 150 itself was "ridiculous" or "absurd" but that the *intent* behind that sentence—to put a financial fraudster of such magnitude away for a considerable period of time, which given his age was tantamount to a life sentence—was not inconceivable. When asked about the sentence, for example, Anton Antonowicz of the *Daily Mirror* commented:

> It's meaningless once you tell a man in his seventies . . . it's twenty-five years, fifty years, or one hundred and fifty . . . I didn't really think too much about it. It was just simply the fact that, alright!, we've had enough of this man, we're going to eradicate him from society.

Alexandra Frean of the *Times* gave personal support to Madoff's sentence, and called attention to the potential deterrent effect of such a punishment, as well as its symbolic importance:

> I think he should be in prison for the rest of his life. They could have said forty years and people probably would have been satisfied, because it's a bit superfluous, to give over one hundred years . . . but I think it was *symbolic and they needed to show they were cracking down.*

Rationales for Harsh Justice

Alexandra Frean's referencing of the symbolic importance of the sentence and her assertion that "they" needed to crack down were typical of the rationales used to justify Madoff's sentence found throughout the coverage. Particularly in the US but also with some emphasis in the UK broadsheets, three key justifications of punishment repeatedly entered the discourse: *symbolism/sending a message, deterrence,* and *retribution.* The Madoff case, once it became a vehicle for discussing and punishing the "anonymous" wrongdoers who had precipitated the financial crisis, had to also include a draconian sentence (for a white-collar crime), not only to give some measure of satisfaction to the victims but also to fulfill the psychosocial function of providing a collective sense of protection, vindication, and catharsis for the crisis and its consequences to society as a whole.

The symbolic rationale for punishment was articulated directly in Judge Chin's statement during the sentencing. As reported in the *New York Times, Daily News, New York Post,* and *Washington Post,* Chin declared that 150 years was indeed intended to be symbolic. Diana Henriques's article for the *New York Times* quoted Chin: "Symbolism is important for at least three reasons . . . retribution, deterrence, and a measure of justice for the victims."[37] Although Chin includes retribution, deterrence, and justice for victims as reason *for* symbolism, I contend that symbolism *itself* became a rationale for punishment in the discourse rather than merely a conduit through which other punishment objectives could be realized. The 150 years was seen as necessary to impart a mythic significance to the punishment; to transform Madoff into even more of an emblem of greed and criminality; and through this mythic punishment to restore the sanctity of the financial system.

Even so, for some the plea and the sentence did not do enough symbolically. In an op-ed, the *Daily News* claimed: "The law says Madoff is eligible for a sentence of 150 years. The number is pure symbolism. It is also disgracefully meager when it is considered against the magnitude of his offenses."[38] Victim Maureen Aebel, in her statement to the court in March 2009, had wanted Judge Chin to reject the plea, and Madoff to go to trial, for the symbolic power it would bring to a case that already had a much broader significance: "If we go to trial, we will show our people in this struggling country and the world, who look to us as the global moral leader, that we hold all people accountable . . . that all crimes including crimes of greed . . . can be punished. And we can demonstrate that we are a country that can learn from our mistakes, and we will be then able to reexamine and improve the mechanisms that exist for our protection that have failed so completely . . . No man, no matter who he knows or who he is able to influence, is above the law." Others felt the sentence itself did not do justice to the scale of the crime.[39]

We have already seen how extensively the media covered the anger of victims, politicians, and the public, and the cries for justice. The second rationale then for Madoff's 150-year punishment—retribution—did not always need to be specifically referenced or discussed per se for its importance in the discourse or in my interviews with journalists and editors in order to be communicated. James Bone of the London *Times* noted:

> The comeuppance of a rich crook is always an emotionally satisfying story, so [the sentence] was obviously emotionally satisfying for all his victims. You saw Elie Wiesel—I mean, basically he wanted to almost torture Madoff!

John Marzulli of the *Daily News*, in reflecting on the anger he witnessed when Ruth Madoff was *not* punished in the same manner as her husband, commented on what he perceived as an American cultural propensity for retributive sentiments: "I think that part of that [desire to see Ruth Madoff punished] is Puritanical—it's part of this country's DNA."

Retribution was not only alluded to or inferred, however. Judge Chin, of course, cited it as one of his reasons for meting out the 150-year sentence. A *New York Times* article which included an interview with Chin about his process of crafting the sentencing statement mentioned how at first Chin neglected to include retribution. But "a defendant should get his just deserts," the judge remembered thinking, and he thus included this rationale.[40] A London *Times* article, citing the need for "just deserts" and retribution, conflated Madoff with the financial crisis, again as we have so often seen, and saddled him with responsibility for creating an existential threat to capitalism: "[Mr. Madoff] may have operated in a world of lies, but his actions will have consequences in the real world. As one observer notes, they have turned a bad year for hedge funds into a catastrophe. They may also sour a generation on the idea of trusting their personal wealth to others. To this extent the Madoff scandal is emblematic of the great crash of 2008 and will need a regulatory response as well as retribution in the courts."[41]

The final rationale given for punishment in the discourse—deterrence—was cited by Chin but also by a wide range of other actors. Victims, lawyers, political figures, and op-ed writers expressed the belief that a 150-year sentence would prevent future frauds from destabilizing the financial system and devastating investors. A *Daily Mirror* op-ed asserted, "The lengthy prison sentence . . . should . . . serve as a warning to any swindler looking to get rich quick on the misery of others."[42] The *Daily News* cited New York City mayor Michael Bloomberg: "Life imprisonment sends a message to other white collar criminals. 'Vengeance is one thing but it's making sure that other people understand that they can't go out and ruin peoples' lives and take away their things.'"[43] Jerry Reisman, an attorney for the victims, posited, "The sentence must be deterrence to others,"[44] while assistant US attorney Marc Litt was quoted in the *New York Times* endorsing "a term that would assure that Madoff will remain in prison for life and forcefully would promote general deterrence."[45] Cynthia Friedman, a victim, even told the *New York Times* prior to the verdict, "We're hoping for a big sentence *only* as a deterrent."[46] In doing so, she downplayed the other rationales, although the retributive tone of much of the victims' testimony suggested deterrence was not the sole motive.

Peter Henning, contributor to the *New York Times*'s DealBook, offered the only opinion to counter the narrative of deterrence as a rationale for punishment in his article "Long Sentences Send a Message Few May Hear." He wrote: "No one in an executive suite views himself as the next Bernie Madoff . . . What happened to [him] is unlikely to have much, if any, deterrent value."[47] And indeed, the long list of Ponzi scheme artists who bilked investors of millions *following* Madoff's sentence bears up Henning's claim. To give but a few examples where charges were filed for Ponzis in 2010–13, Nevin Shapiro of Capitol Investments USA in 2010 was charged with orchestrating a $900 million Ponzi, for which he received twenty years in prison; also in 2010, Lydia Cladek was indicted for operating her investment company as a Ponzi scheme with losses of $100 million, and received a sentence of thirty years; and in 2012, Brendan Coughlin of Provident Royalties, LLC, was indicted for a $485 million Ponzi, for which he would serve fewer than two years.[48]

Moreover, there is some evidence that white-collar sentences are harsher during periods of crisis or scandal but then return to less punitive levels following these scandals, thus neutralizing a deterrent effect through inconsistent application of punishment. In her "Sentencing Corporate Crime: Responses to Scandal and Sarbanes-Oxley,"[49] although she does not look at individual offenders like Madoff, Miranda Galvin concludes that corporations sentenced during the period of accounting scandals in the early 2000s (the notorious Enron and WorldCom scandals, for example) had an increased likelihood of receiving harsh fines due to amplified attention given to white-collar crime by the public, and collective framing of such white-collar crimes as egregious during periods of scandals. Additional data from the Ponzi Tracker database,[50] which includes all Ponzis uncovered from 2009 to 2013, revealed wide disparities in sentencing for offenders per million dollars stolen. In 2011, for instance, Jason Severs was given a sentence of 300 months, or 218 months per million he stole ($1.37 million). That same year, James Fry was given 204 months, or .06 months per million (in his case for $3.65 billion stolen). Obviously, multiple factors influence sentencing decisions. However, if the claim is being made that a harsh sentence will act as a deterrent, one would expect less capricious patterns to be key to the message delivered. The level of arbitrariness involved in the punishment of financial crimes is so high that a sentence like Madoff's is analogous to the odds of winning the lottery. It is also worth noting that long sentences may be especially *ineffective* in deterring financial crimes: given the penchant with which those in finance thrive on risk taking and gambling, these are odds they will continue to play.

Discipline and Punish! ... But Not the Stock Market

Each of the rationales for punishment found in the discourse described here relates to the deeply felt need to take action against dynamics which led to the crisis. The performance of exiling Madoff for more than a lifetime may have satisfied immediate, collective, and individual psychological needs; yet two important elements were missing from the discussion: the discourse surrounding sentencing lacked a structural critique of how free-market capitalism incubates the conditions under which frauds are likely to occur and are even commonplace. It also lacked an acknowledgment of the way Madoff deflected attention away from the wrongdoing—criminal or merely nefariously unethical—that bore *direct* responsibility for the financial crisis.

Remarkably, very little attempt was made or hypotheses offered in the media coverage as to *why* Madoff committed the crime. As such, conversations about possible structural influences were muted. To ask this question, perhaps, would have been to appear too empathetic toward a man who had earned universal condemnation. Such a question, in itself, became political. Madoff was "evil" and a "monster" or "the Devil" besot with greed. Unlike a violent crime or "street" crime committed by a person of more limited means, where intense focus is often placed on personal, psychological, and structural factors that may have caused the person to offend, with someone like Madoff—a man of power, privilege, and considerable wealth who came from a traditional middle-class family—explanatory theories were not offered. "Mitigating factors" would have been met with laughter and derision. What mitigating factors could there possibly be for a man who had his own jet and stole from pension funds and charities?

Yet without attempting to understand why someone would engage in this level of deceit, however odious the crime may be, it is difficult to conjecture whether the threat of harsh punishment would act as an effective deterrent and combat fraud. Why should economic offenders be considered entirely rational actors able to disinterestedly weigh the possibility of lengthy jail time against the possible benefits that might accrue through wrongful actions? Why would they be removed from structural and psychological influences on behavior? An important study on US opinions of white-collar crime published the same year Madoff admitted to his crime, "Public Support for Getting Tough on Corporate Crime: Racial and Political Divides,"[51] offers some empirical evidence for why such little focus was given in the discourse to the question of what led him to offend. The article showed that liberal Americans, who typically attribute crime to external, structural forces and oppression when thinking about street crime, actually *join* their conservative counterparts to "endorse an internal-dispositional attribution style when considering whether corporate offenders should be harshly punished." In other words, liberals, when thinking about white-collar criminals, focus on personal, internal "bad" qualities that led these offenders to deviate. Outside pressures are downplayed. The same repugnance of liberals to policies, say, in the "War on Drugs" that focus on deterrence through long prison sentences rather than habilitation, disappears when contemplating the white-collar offender.

This belief then by liberals and conservatives alike necessarily displaces attention away from systemic problems that might influence white-collar offenders. Solving the problem presented by Bernie Madoff by giving him a Methuselah-worthy sentence fits in entirely with this ideological configuration, which creates an impediment to fully understanding why financial crime occurs. Paradoxes, then, emerge. In "Public Support for Getting Tough on Corporate Crime," the results indicated that although, as the top figure on the next page indicates, an overwhelming majority of Americans (77.7%) support harsher penalties for corporate criminals, at the same time 59 percent of respondents believe that *less* regulation of the stock market is needed (bottom figure). Indeed, only a third of respondents would support more regulation.

As the authors conclude, this paradox "may well indicate that most Americans have faith in capitalism and are generally reluctant to embrace the notion of increasing governmental regulation." Another conclusion we can draw from this is that Americans believe that deterrence can be achieved and crises avoided by incarcerating *individuals* rather than changing a system that makes greed "good" and incentivizes risk-taking behavior in an environment where the likelihood of getting

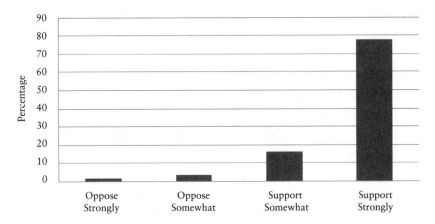

US public support for tougher penalties for corporate executives.
Data source: Unnever, Benson, and Cullen, "Public Support for
Getting Tough on Corporate Crime."

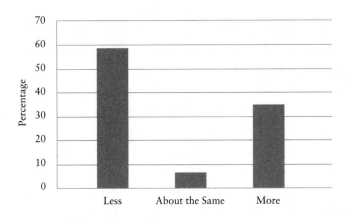

US public support for regulating the stock market.
Data source: Unnever, Benson, and Cullen, "Public
Support for Getting Tough on Corporate Crime."

"caught" remains small. Unfortunately, corresponding data are not available for the United Kingdom. However, given the very similar discourses in the coverage and interviews, as well as the political and social convergence that has taken place, there is little reason to think that the UK public holds significantly different opinions on this matter from its US counterpart.

This paradox (the public's wish to control and punish white-collar crime alongside its refusal to consider proactive measures like increased regulation) should make us think twice about the supposed public utility of Madoff's 150-year sentence; in this light, the sentence does not (as many at the time claimed) rebuke the malpractices that led to the financial crisis. After all, Ponzi schemes like his, or Allen Stanford's seven-billion-dollar fraud, did not cause, but were exposed through the crisis. The reality of a system that fostered the criminality or legal but highly unethical practices was not addressed or attacked through Madoff's incarceration. The declaration of a symbolic victory following his sentencing lumped together his Ponzi with all the other lightly regulated Wall Street practices that had fostered profit mongering at any cost; but it did not admit that the fundamental conditions that led to both the crisis and the Ponzi remained unchanged. My conversation with Diana Henriques touched on this issue of misguided symbolism:

> Early on, a common comment was that Madoff was just part of the same, that he was one of those Wall Street crooks. And maybe not even the worst of the Wall Street crooks. I mean, the *real* Wall Street crooks were the head of J.P. Morgan and the heads of big banks. I would invariably meet people who wanted to make that paradigm, that Madoff was an example of Wall Street's betrayal of America. Well, Madoff was a Wall Street figure, he did betray everyone who trusted him. But you would never have made that connection but for the correlation in time.

Even if all the frauds that contributed to the crisis (of which Ponzi schemes were not necessarily a part) were prosecuted, what the Financial Crisis Inquiry Commission termed "fatal flaws" in the system would continue to lay the groundwork for crises to come. The commission pointed out how these flaws, like excessive borrowing, reckless risk taking in investments, lack of transparency, failures in regulation and deregulation, and "a systemic breakdown in accountability and ethics," were among the key factors that led to the crisis. In looking at the financial crisis of 2008, it is extraordinary that no high-level executives were prosecuted. This dearth becomes even more shocking (and frightening) when we recall that the savings and loan scandal of the 1980s produced over eight hundred successful prosecutions (including the high-profile conviction of Charles Keating for fraud, racketeering, and conspiracy[52]) and that these hefty prosecutions did not prevent the accounting scandals of the late 1990s and early 2000s, nor the financial crisis of 2008. "A crisis of this magnitude cannot be the work of a few bad actors," the Financial Crisis Inquiry Commission wrote, "and such was not the case here . . . We do place special responsibility with the public leaders charged with protecting our financial system, those entrusted to run our regulatory agencies, and the chief executives of companies whose failures drove us to crisis . . . but as a nation, we must also accept responsibility for what we permitted to occur. Collectively, but certainly not unanimously, we acquiesced to or embraced a system, a set of policies and actions, that gave rise to our present predicament."[53]

White-collar Crimes by Any Other Name

In prison, Bernie Madoff has cultivated a curious relationship with individual journalists in the media. On the one hand, he has declared his repugnance of the entire industry due to its treatment of his family (particularly his sons but also his wife and his brother, Peter) as well as himself and the case generally. In one of our first exchanges, he provided "background information regarding [his] past experiences with the media and why [he] rejected continuing a dialogue with them." He gave me a thorough accounting of his interactions with the press which would explain the alleged rejection:

> At the moment of my arrest I was instructed by my attorneys to make no comments to the media about anything, which I followed and only fueled their anger and speculation. My face quickly appeared on the cover of New York Magazine as the Joker character with the caption of MONSTER. The article was a scathing assortment of lies . . . A feeding frenzy of the media began and they camped outside my apartment house waiting for me to jump out of the window. Every network positioned their satellite trucks outside making it impossible for my wife to leave the house.

His experience when he arrived at prison did not improve the interactions:

The *NY Post* as well as *NY Magazine* had sent letters to all the inmates solicit-ing ANY stories about me for payment to their commissary accounts (clearly illegal). Knowing this, they started to give the bribes to the inmates' family who could then send the money to the inmates. As expected, this started a flurry of misinformation and fantastic stories . . . The information that constantly ap-peared in the press was so distorted and vicious.

In spite of these complaints and initial insistence that he has rejected dialogue with the media, he has made presumable exceptions to this rule. Among the journalists and media personalities he granted on-the-record interviews to are Diana Henriques of the *New York Times*, David Gelles and Gillian Tett of the *Financial Times*, Charles Gaspa-rino of *Fox Business*, Barbara Walters of *20/20*, Steve Fishman of *New York Magazine*, and Sital Patel of the *Wall Street Journal*. As Gelles and Tett observed in their "From Behind Bars, Madoff Spins His Story," "He clearly hopes to have a hand in shaping his legacy." These interviews did not always produce the version of the story he wanted conveyed and sometimes the interviewers overtly challenged Madoff's assertions as mendacious.[54]

Not to be deterred, select members of the media whom he declared atypical of their profession (and thus worthy of interaction) continue to be inducted into an opaque virtual network maintained by Madoff through the prison e-mail system. The opacity resides in Madoff's use of the blind copy function: when he sends a message to the group, in-dividual members are unable to see who else has been included in the chain. It is unknown how many have been included in this network or who else might be included other than members of the media. There is an ironic parallel between the aura of exclusivity fostered in his fraud and the aura of exclusivity maintained here. Madoff declared members of the media in this group "different" and excluded them from his general criticisms leveled at the media. Through the network, Madoff has again become a sought-after "expert," using the celebrity achieved this time not through market wizardry but through the mas-sive fraud which continues to fascinate the public and hence attract reporters.

The missives Madoff has sent from prison often take a professorial tone, that of an expert commenter: he is giving a self-described "lesson" on currency arbitrage or the history of decimalization, sounding notes of caution about dark pools, expounding on the victim recovery efforts by the trustee Irving Picard, or contesting the loss amounts of his fraud cited by the press and Picard. Another thread of Madoff's letters to the media, though, tapped into sentiments that blossomed into full popular expression during the Occupy Wall Street protest movement starting in September 2011: namely, a sense of a double standard and injustice in the lack of punishment of the wrongdoing at the major financial institutions in sharp contrast to the punishment that he, as an individual, received. Of course, Madoff's presenting this comparison for journalists cannot be extricated from the self-interested motive of, as Gelles and Tett termed it, "spinning his story."

Notwithstanding this spin, Madoff's critique (to members of the media) of the differential punishment of white-collar criminality at the individual versus institutional level and its reportage served, ironically, to inject systemic, structural concerns into the discourse by juxtaposing his case against the wrongdoing which led to the crisis. In a sense, just as the media and public conflated his case with the crisis, through these conversations he also drew parallels but for the purpose of showing the disparities in sentencing (or lack thereof).

One of the comparisons Madoff drew was between the charges filed against his brother, lawyer Peter Madoff (former chief compliance officer and senior managing director at Madoff's firm), the sentence handed down, and the dearth of prosecution of the CEOs of Goldman Sachs and Lehman Brothers. After pleading guilty, Peter was sentenced to ten years in federal prison in December 2012 and ordered to forfeit an almost fantastical sum of $146 billion, which prosecutors alleged was the total paid by investors into BLMIS from 1996 to 2008.[55] His admitted crimes included mail and wire fraud, falsifying documents, tax fraud, conspiracy to commit securities fraud, and even paying his wife for a job she never performed. Brother Bernie would write:

What is unbelievable is that my brother who was forced to accept a plea of guilty to what really is a charge of bookkeeping errors of judgment as well as signing off on my investment advisors application that included information supplied by me with the advice of my attorneys (ex SEC directors)—this was considered a criminal offense. He also said he had zero knowledge of my Ponzi scheme and was not charged [with that offense]. Now compare this to that of all the other CEO's of Goldman and Lehman, to name a few, [who] also signed off on their firms' financial and compliance fillings and made the successful claim that they relied on others that the information was correct. WHAT IS WRONG WITH THIS PICTURE???

Peter Madoff's claim to be ignorant of Bernie's Ponzi even as he knowingly attempted to deceive the Securities and Exchange Commission, certifying false investment results and working closely with Bernie for forty years, was generally met with incredulity. He "enabled" the scheme, as FBI director Janice Fedarcyk described.[56] Bernie Madoff's motives for shielding his brother, guilty or not, are obvious. However, the comparison made with Goldman Sachs does have legitimate parallels. In 2010 the iconic investment bank was forced by the SEC to pay a $550 million fine, the largest in the history of the SEC. Goldman, in a civil case, was charged with fraud for in 2007 peddling to investors a collateralized debt obligation (CDO) comprising subprime mortgages known as "ABACUS 2007-AC1," without disclosing to them that the product was designed to fail by hedge fund manager John Paulson, who along with Goldman Sachs took a short position against those same subprime mortgage assets, betting on the collapse of the housing market.[57] The subprime mortgage market did indeed tank, and by October 2007, 99 percent of the ABACUS assets had been downgraded, causing investors massive losses[58] but resulting in a billion-dollar profit for Paulson and millions in fees for Goldman. As the SEC would itself declare, no one at Goldman was held individually accountable; no one went to prison. The bank was allowed to pay the fine, a fraction of its total net earnings that year of $8.35 billion[59] without admitting to any wrongdoing, as the Department of Justice decided not to pursue criminal charges.

In the words of Senator Carl Levin (D-MI), who presided over the Senate permanent subcommittee investigating the financial crisis, at which Goldman CEO Lloyd Blankfein testified: "Investment banks such as Goldman Sachs were not simply market-makers, they were self-interested promoters of risky and complicated schemes that helped trigger the Crisis . . . They bundled toxic mortgages into complex financial instruments, got the credit ratings agencies to label them AAA securities, and sold them to investors, magnifying and spreading risk throughout the financial system, and all too often betting against the instruments they sold and profiting at the expense of their clients."[60] If an individual like Peter Madoff was being held accountable through imprisonment for actions that "enabled" Madoff's Ponzi but were unrelated to the financial crisis, it would seem that much more important for those who knowingly "enabled" practices that directly led to the crisis to be punished. Madoff would go on in a letter to remark about the Goldman case:

> When you see a situation like [theirs] where the products were actually designed to fail and everyone had to know this, then there is no excuse for no prosecution. The problem is that this is not a new or even recent culture. I don't think it is necessary to give you the numerous examples of the lack of reporting exposing the corruption of the Global banking industry or Wall Street in general with little if any prosecution other than low level employees. Is it really possible that all of this fraud went on without the senior people of these institutions not being aware of it?

Two additional cases Madoff latched onto as exemplary of double standards in reportage and punishment for wrongdoing exposed approximately the same time as his Ponzi involved another megabank, the British HSBC, and the London Interbank Offered Rate (LIBOR) scandal, which involved multiple banks including Citigroup, Barclays, J.P. Morgan, Deutsche Bank, UBS, and the Royal Bank of Scotland. "I guess they are not as interesting as Madoff," he would cynically note in comparing the public outcry and media attention paid to his case, going on to elaborate:

> You are aware of the reports of the HSBC settlements of 1.9 billion concerning their charges of fraud in money laundering and sanction issue violations (too big to jail). Add to this the recently announced UBS 1.5 billion settlement

and admission to fraud concerning LIBOR manipulation. They are the first with more banks to certainly follow. It is important to realize that the financial damage done to the public in both cases in dollar terms is greater than that done in the Madoff Ponzi scheme. As you certainly know, every loan [to] every individual or institution is in fact set and therefore negatively impacted by LIBOR. The same damage can be said of the fraud that HSBC committed. Now consider the important fact that the actual financial loss suffered by Madoff victims will be insignificant if anything at all when the recoveries are complete . . . There will be no recovery of loss to the victims of the HSBC and LIBOR frauds. Equally important is the fact that I am serving a 150 year sentence and the other crimes went unpunished by jail sentences.

Again Madoff's motive for bringing these cases to the attention of his inside group of journalists and media personalities may be far from altruistic. It can even be seen as a technique of neutralization for his own crime, a "condemnation of the condemners" for their hypocrisy.[61] But undeniable is his charge that public and media attention was comparatively missing in the treatment of the British HSBC and LIBOR scandals, in spite of the severity of the charges and the implications for the global financial system.

LIBOR, the benchmark international interest rate for short-term borrowing among institutional investors, is fundamental to borrowers at every level because hundreds of trillions in loans (both commercial and consumer) and other investments are linked to it. It also is supposed to provide a diagnostic snapshot of the health of the banking system.[62] Since the rate is determined by a panel of banks that submit subjective, "good faith" estimates of the lowest interest rate they believe they could obtain from other banks, trust is presumed and essential. In 2008, however, widespread manipulation of the LIBOR rate was exposed, revealing that traders and managers in the major international banks, including the Royal Bank of Scotland, Deutsche Bank, Bank of America, J.P. Morgan, Barclays, UBS, Credit Suisse, Citigroup, HSBC, and Société Générale, were deliberately underreporting their rates in order to create the impression that they were more financially sound than they actually were, and to increase profits.[63] In the course of the investigation, rampant collusion among the firms' employees was iden-tified, with online chat rooms, shamelessly dubbed "the Cartel" and "the Mafia" and the "Bandits Club," serving as meeting places.[64]

The LIBOR manipulation was far from a victimless crime. Fannie Mae and Freddie Mac lost up to three billion dollars, according to the *Washington Post*. British housing minister Grant Shapps in 2012 went so far as to link the scandal with home repossession following the credit crisis: "All the research into homelessness proves that there are a lot of different causes, of which the LIBOR rate may have [been] a contribu-tory factor, if indeed it transpires that mortgage rates have been adjusted as a result," he stated.[65] And not to be taken lightly were the more ab-stract consequences, including eroding trust in the global financial mar-kets, consequences that were invoked in the Madoff case.

Although not in the same way directly linked to the financial cri-sis, HSBC's "misconduct" during this time period was immense; the consequences of this misconduct were far-reaching and could be seen as contributing to the erosion of trust. In a damning three-hundred-page US Senate report covering the years 2001 to 2010, the bank was found to have violated OFAC[66] sanctions and illegally conducted tens of thousands of transactions for customers in the high-risk countries of Iran, Libya, Sudan, Cuba, and Burma, thus "facilitating transactions on behalf of terrorists, drug traffickers and other wrongdoers." It also maintained business with the Saudi Al Rajhi Bank, a firm with links to terrorism in the years following September 11, and allowed (through American HSBC subsidiaries) for the laundering of billions of dollars from violent Mexican drug cartels linked to countless killings.

The consequences for HSBC, and its executives particularly, stand in stark contrast to those faced by Madoff, even as it showed itself to be swimming in blood-tainted funds. Rather than face criminal prosecu-tion, it entered into a deferred prosecution deal with the Manhattan Dis-trict Attorney and the Department of Justice, paying a $1.9 billion fine[67] and promising to "behave" over the next five years while beefing up its internal regulations. No top HSBC officials faced charges or the threat of prison as they admitted to their "mistakes." Those banks involved in the LIBOR-fixing scandal were similarly forced to pay billions in fines through settlements with British and US regulators. However, Madoff was incorrect in stating that these crimes went unpunished. Twenty-two people, primarily nonexecutive-level traders, will face trial, although under the threat of much shorter sentences.[68]

Just a Ritual?

Although there is no unified sociological perspective on punishment, one of its key perspectives, provided by Emile Durkheim, is useful in unpacking the significance of the Bernie Madoff case in the sociohistorical context of the financial crisis. For Durkheim, punishment is not primarily functional in its ability to incapacitate or even to directly deter would-be criminals. Rather it enhances social solidarity by stirring strong collective emotions against the wrongdoer, thereby uniting the group around the accepted moral order, preserving that order. As sociologist David Garland describes, for Durkheim, punishment is "an expressive institution: a realm for ritualized expression of social values and controlled release of psychic energy . . . The rituals are directed less at the individual offender than at the audience of impassioned onlookers whose cherished values and security had been momentarily undermined by the offender's actions."[69] With the benefit of distance from the immediacy of the crisis and the sensation of the Madoff case, the discourses surrounding his sentencing and punishment reveal the emotive role it served, providing the publics in both America and Britain with an individual whose epic crime ensnared thousands, from celebrities to firefighters, making him an ideal subject on which to project anger and anxiety about the world-order-as-we-know-it crumbling around them. It was necessary for Madoff to be labeled the Devil in order to sanctify and protect the financial system, which relies so heavily on trust and an implicit faith in a steady and sure invisible hand. The elation felt when he was sentenced went far beyond happiness that his victims alone received a measure of justice; it was also a sense that some karmic order had been restored: one of those elitist Wall Street types who had plunged the world into recession was going to die in prison.

If the punishment in the Madoff case had only provided a symbolic resolution to the ethical problems and criminality which led to the crisis—a temporary moment of social solidarity—its impact would have faded soon after the sentence was read. However, it also provoked reflection on issues which could inspire transformation: the inequalities between the treatment of elite offenders and street offenders, gaping disparities in wealth even among victims, the fraudulent acquisition of wealth, and the farcical regulation of the financial sector. The moment of crisis was also the moment of opportunity. During this time it was impossible to exaggerate the dangers of runaway "casino capitalism." The home equity and livelihoods of millions of working families had disappeared. At the same time, the makers of the maelstrom were vulnerable. But because of the lack of a sustained critique of structural forces, perhaps because of limits within our own collective consciousness, even the discourses about Madoff, whether victorious or vindictive, overwhelmingly failed to propose alternatives other than more ameliorative versions of the status quo. This silence was (and remains) so thick that even an international movement, Occupy Wall Street, was unable to make broad or systemic changes that would negate the possibility of another crisis. We as a society ultimately acquiesced and helped the culprits back to their feet, after which they dusted themselves off and returned to business as usual.

6 THE MORE THINGS CHANGE, THE MORE THEY REMAIN THE SAME?

In the midst of a crisis, it is hard to see where the exit might be. Crises are not singular events. While they have obvious triggers, the tectonic shifts they represent take many years to work out.

—David Harvey

There's that line from the Talmud . . . such is the punishment of a liar, that even when he tells the truth, no one listens.

—Deborah Margolin, playwright, *Imagining Madoff*

THE FINANCIAL CRISIS of 2007–9 and Bernie Madoff's crisis have passed. No tectonic rumbles of the same magnitude have since stirred the economic and social landscape, but these events are still well within our collective rearview mirror, specters reminding us of those days of shock and uncertainty, muted promises of perhaps more to come. Like existential crises impelling urgent reevaluations of life with the intent of discovering its core meaning and purpose, these two intertwined crises had a similar psychosocial effect. Faith in the system was rocked, and evaluative questions rose to the surface. Writing in that moment in 2010, anthropologist David Harvey in *The Enigma of Capital and the Crises of Capitalism* declared with cautious optimism, "Crises are moments of paradox and possibility out of which all manner of alternatives, including socialist and anti-capitalist ones can spring."[1] In this final chapter, I evaluate the legacy of the social impact of the Madoff case. It may seem that complete cynicism is warranted on the basis of the fallout. First, I describe what changed after Madoff and the crisis, namely a growing awareness of class inequalities, manifested through Occupy and in mainstream US and UK politics. Next, however, I detail how much has remained the same: displacing blame for systemic problems onto individuals, the use of punishment as panacea for systemic issues, minimalist regulation that encourages financial risk taking at the expense of the taxpayer, and timid journalistic approaches to white-collar crime. With these impediments to change, I propose a central role for journalists and social scientists in bringing to the public a deeper understanding of financial crime and those who engage in such crimes, an understanding that brings structure to the forefront but also does not neglect the human and that recognizes all "monsters" as our own creations.

What Changed?

As described in Chapter 4, a newly awakened consciousness of class and social inequality—and indeed anger—brewed in the wake of the Madoff Ponzi. In the United States particularly, where class distinctions have been denied by an individualist meritocratic ideology, this was an unexpected development. This anger and awareness would not find full expression for several years after Madoff's incarceration. But when it did, the effects would be felt worldwide and would ripple through the next decade on the political stage.

In September 2011, the "Occupy Wall Street" movement spilled onto the streets of New York City after the Canadian activist *Adbusters* magazine issued a call to "flood into lower Manhattan, set up tents, kitchens, peaceful barricades and occupy Wall Street."[2] On September 17, two thousand protesters arrived in New York City's financial district, and hundreds set up camp in the privately owned Zuccotti Park (dubbed "Liberty Park"). They would establish direct, consensus-based democratic practices[3] through general assembly meetings, and over one hundred working groups organized a variety of actions and activities, including marches to Wall Street, educational "teach-ins," production of the *Occupied Wall Street Journal*, music and arts projects, the provision of medical care, a kitchen, a library, sanitation, and safety. They remained until November, when the NYPD, wearing riot gear and arresting those who would not comply, forcibly evicted them from the park. However, by that time hundreds of occupations had blossomed in cities across the United States, in Britain with "Occupy the London

Stock Exchange," and around the world. Protests linked to Occupy were witnessed in 951 cities and 82 countries that October.[4] The Occupiers' framing of the malaises, confronting so many as the consequence of the "1%" profiting at the expense of the "99%," had wide resonance.

In explaining the success of Occupy and the motivations of those who participated, Kalle Lasn, cofounder of *Adbusters*, gave this account: "There's a very visceral anger against the financial community. Many people feel that these people who are financial fraudsters, who basically got away with it, have yet to be brought to justice. It seems like we the people now have to congregate on Wall Street and other financial districts around the world and force the global economic system to move in a better, more just direction."[5] In a study of Occupy, sociologist Ruth Milkman examined the primary issues that led participants to support the movement. Nearly 50 percent indicated "inequality/the 1%." The next most frequently cited reasons were "money in politics/frustration with D.C." (25.5%) and "corporate greed" (18.5%), revealing the degree to which an economic system that privileged the advancement of the few at the expense of the masses had taken center stage in a new national and international debate. "It names the source of the crisis: The problems of the 99% are caused by Wall Street greed, corrupt banks, and corporate take-over of the political system."[6]

The Occupiers did not present any formalized demands with their collective concerns—a controversial strategy. However, their "Declaration of the Occupation of New York City," the first official collective statement of the Occupiers of Zuccotti Park, articulated some of their grievances: "We write so that all people who feel wronged by the corporate forces of the world can know that we are your allies," it proclaimed, and listed twenty-three "charges" against the corporate-government nexus, including, "They have taken bailouts from taxpayers with impunity, and continue to give executives bonuses," and, "They determine economic policy, despite the catastrophic failures their policies have produced and continue to produce."[7] In October, Occupy London protesters camping outside of St. Paul's Cathedral similarly agreed to an "Initial Statement." "We refuse to pay for the banks' crises," they demanded. "We do not accept the cuts as either necessary or inevitable. We demand an end to the global tax injustice and our democracy representing corporations instead of the people," adding, "We want regulators to be genuinely independent of the industries they regulate," underscoring the common crisis-related themes driving the movement overseas.

Those who have analyzed the consequences of the Occupy movement have frequently cited its influence on national and international discourse. "Occupy transformed U.S. political discourse. It elevated the issue of growing economic inequality to the center of public attention . . . to a degree unprecedented in recent public memory, social class became a central focus of political debate," Milkman argues, noting how news media during the occupation of Zuccotti Park focused heavily on inequality: "Although the media attention did subside after the eviction, the broader political discourse continues to be peppered with ongoing references to 'the 1%.'" Sarah Van Gelder of *YES! Magazine* claims: "Occupy Wall Street has already accomplished something that changes everything. It has fundamentally altered the national conversation." She cites Paul Krugman: "A group of people started camping out in Zuccotti Park, and all of a sudden, the conversation started being about the right things."[8]

Occupy Wall Street's framing of the fundamental problems with government and the economy as rooted in the greed and power of the "1%" certainly provided the media and public with language that could unite a broad range of concerns. Yet as my content analysis of the Madoff media coverage indicated, issues of inequality and social class were *already* becoming a large part of the discourse at least two years before the Zuccotti encampments. Consciousness had already awakened, and the Madoff case played the role of catalyst. Occupy Wall Street facilitated broader understanding in part because it lacked specificity; it did not rely on symbolic offenders such as Madoff to exemplify the problems it identified. The problems, for Occupy, were rooted in a pathological structure, were more abstract and conceptual, and incapable of being solved by the imprisonment of one offender or the meeting of a single list of demands.

Awareness of class-based inequality and anger was not quashed with the disassembling of the Occupy camps, which also had repercussions for US and UK politics. Populist appeals were strongly evident in the 2016 US presidential campaign cycle, particularly in candidate Senator Bernie Sanders's unexpectedly strong campaign, which appealed to the "99%." In an introduction to his political platform, he wrote: "Do we continue the 40-year decline of our middle class and the growing gap between the very rich and everyone else, or do we fight for a progressive economic agenda that creates jobs, raises wages, protects the environment and provides health care for all? Are we prepared to take on the enormous economic and political power of the billionaire class, or do we continue to slide into economic and political oligarchy?"[9]

A resurgence of class-centered politics was not limited to the American left. The same resentments that contributed to the success of Bernie Sanders can also be seen as producing his antithesis on the right, Donald Trump, or the "Brexit" in the United Kingdom after primarily working-class, white voters in England opted overwhelmingly to leave the European Union. The right's displacement of anger, evident in these events, onto targets such as Muslims and immigrants unfortunately leads us to conclude that however much Madoff and the financial crisis led, temporarily, to openness to a different perspective, the window quickly was shut, and much too much has remained the same.

What Remained the Same?

Occupy Wall Street was more successful in moving the conversation about the financial crisis to broader structural concerns about inequality than had been evinced in the conversations about the Madoff case. Yet even with their structural critique, the protestors' vision of how to effectively deal with the 1%, and with the criminal 1% (the difference between these two categories remaining blurry in the protests), was expressed at times as it was with Madoff: as a desire for harsher punishment and imprisonment of a specific elite group. "Millions of underwater homeowners have paid the price for Wall Street's crimes. From mortgage fraud to predatory lending, it's time to put bankers in jail," an article on OccupyWallStreet.net affirmed. "The time is now for Congress and the Obama administration to make Wall Street pay us back: Prosecute Wall Street bankers for stealing our homes, savings and livelihood."[10] Variations of "Jail the bankers!" and "Arrest the bankers" or even "Hungry? Eat a banker" appeared on signs carried at Occupy demonstrations.[11] The *New York Times* DealBook article "On Wall Street, a Protest Matures" cited Occupiers including the cofounder of Code Pink—an organization dedicated to ending US wars and militarism—whose demands included prison time for bankers: "I think a good deal of bankers should be in jail," one commented, while a video of Roseanne Barr advocating for a return of the guillotine for guilty bankers was played to entertain a group of protestors.[12] In the survey issued by Milkman to Occupiers at Zuccotti Park, which asked for the main issues of concern to them, although 50 percent indicated that "inequality/the 1%" led them to Occupy, only 9.2 percent indicated that "capitalism as a system" was their top concern. Identifying the "1%" as the overriding concern, even though capitalism as a system was also a lesser concern, shows how the movement lacked clear alternatives to the structural elements of the economic system, which lead to ever-increasing inequality, debt, foreclosures, the creation of risky financial products, and the incestuous relationship between government and business. The punishment of the 1%, the bankers, became a way to focus anger when the real target—an entire financial system—was so abstract.

The retributive impulse for punishment after Madoff and the financial crisis went far beyond the confines of the Occupy movement.[13] Lack of any punishment made these cries all the more pointed. Although federal prosecutions have been successful in over a thousand criminal cases related to the crisis,[14] these were "mostly small fry." The lack of prosecution of high-level executives, "targeting down," and "too big to jail" displayed a remarkable tone-deaf double standard of justice. The US attorney's office reported in 2012 that still, even postcrisis, only 9 percent of federal criminal cases filed were for white-collar offenses,[15] and less than 1 percent of those serving time in federal prison were there for these crimes.[16] Further, of the 2,948 people in the United States who were given life sentences from 1999 to 2011 for nonviolent crimes, a meager 4 of these were for white-collar offenses, or approximately 0.1 percent of those sentences.[17] Even some critical criminologists, who have extensively critiqued using the criminal justice system as a way of dealing with social problems, have advocated for more criminalization when dealing with economic crimes.[18] They maintain that criminalization would help in politicizing white-collar crime, and consequently would displace the disproportionate attention given to street crime.

There are several significant problems with these widespread narratives that suggest "Jail the bankers" would make progress in preventing another financial crisis from occurring or in reducing social, economic, or racial inequalities. We have seen a consistency in the narratives of the Madoff and other cases, advocating for more jail time for economic offenses: remove failed regulators to fix regulation; remove Madoff types to stop greed; target the 1% to stop inequality. While appearing to make radical claims, these propositions actually bolster the framework in place. To focus on individual economic criminals or on those who make over a certain income seeks to superficially resolve the problems of capitalism within the frameworks *created by* capitalism, frameworks that include the extant criminal justice system. This is not to say that wrongdoers do not, from a retributive standpoint, deserve to be punished for the harm they caused, or that this would not feel good. But to suggest that incarceration would lead to anything other than a slightly more equitable percentage of "token" white-collar offenders is misguided. Some scholars have argued that white-collar criminals would be more responsive to efforts at deterrence because these crimes are more rational. "Economic offending is more calculative than conventional crime, involves a greater element of rational planning," an article in *Critical Criminology* claims. Yet there is no evidence that more criminalization would actually work as a deterrent. Criminologist David Weisburd's study of white-collar offenders[19] concluded just the opposite: they were *not* deterred through stints in prison, just as the War on Drugs has not deterred drug use and sales.

A further problem with the impulse to punish individual offenders like Madoff are the assumptions made by the public, the media, and some scholars about the factors that lead to the offense. Michael Levi points out, "The media and corporate and political commentators typically discuss white-collar crimes and corporate corruption as 'rotten apple' cases"[20] versus "rotten barrels."[21] Supporting this claim, "Public Support for Getting Tough on Corporate Crime: Political and Racial Divides" demonstrates that even those who lean liberal attribute to financial fraudsters some kind of internal dispositional flaw that leads them to offend, while they see the causes of conventional crime rooted more in external factors like poverty and oppression.[22] The financial criminal is presented in a way as someone whose wrongdoing occurs outside of a sociohistoric context and whose motives can be reduced to greed or malice without any attempt to understand the structural, psychological, or emotional factors involved. And as these kinds of crimes are committed by the more affluent, it is politically permissible and even *expected* for liberals and progressives to advocate for harsh punishment.

Amid continued calls for punishment and expressions of astonishment that—other than Madoff, who was not responsible for the crisis—no Wall Street figures had gone to jail, something else had also quietly, surreptitiously been returning to the pre-Madoff status quo: the state of governmental regulation of the markets. Historian Philip Mirowski, in *Never Let a Serious Crisis Go to Waste*, assessed the aftermath of the events of 2007–9 as "The Crisis That Didn't Change Much of Anything" and a "pathetic waste" of an opportunity for change.[23] Indeed, in the ten years since the financial crisis and since whistleblower Harry Markopolos strode in front of Congress and declared the SEC to be "financially illiterate" and in need of an overhaul after the Madoff Ponzi, it is difficult to see signs of substantive regulatory change. Take the Emergency Economic Stabilization Act of 2008. Initially intended to allow the US government to buy toxic mortgages from banks and unfreeze the credit markets, its Troubled Asset Relief Program (TARP) would be redeployed through the Capital Purchase Program to quickly inject $250 billion of equity directly into the banks. They were thus bailed out in highly favorable terms. Programs for average Americans like the Hardest Hit Fund, by contrast, stingily gave out a fraction of their resources over prolonged periods of time.[24] The former special investigator general in charge of the oversight of TARP, Neil Barofsky, would write in his exposé *Bailout*, "We found . . . the placement of the interests of the too-big-to-fail financial institutions and their executives above those of the taxpayers funding their bailouts."[25] Beyond the billions authorized under TARP, largely overlooked by the media was the Government Accounting Office's audit of the Federal Reserve's "emergency" lending that indicated over sixteen trillion dollars were secretly channeled to domestic and international banks,[26] even as the working and middle class faced unemployment, eviction, and foreclosure without assistance. So much for regulating the banks: this sent the message that ignoring regulation would be rewarded.

The Dodd-Frank Wall Street Reform and Consumer Protection Act, which passed in 2010 in response to public outcry, did have positive outcomes such as the creation of the Financial Stability Oversight Council and an independent Bureau of Consumer Financial Protection, but it did not go far enough to eliminate the possibility of another taxpayer bailout of too-big-to-fail institutions.[27] And since its passage, its provisions have been steadily attacked and eroded in Congress by deregulatory factions primarily within the Republican Party.[28] Goldman Sachs and other banks thus have begun surreptitiously selling risky products eerily similar to those implicated in the exacerbation of the crisis, though under different names.[29] Large-scale shifts are not evident. There are the same disproportionate emphases placed on "traditional" crime and crimes of the poor and the same demands for deregulation and laissez-faire capitalism. Diana Henriques would lament after Madoff and the crisis, "Never have I seen financial amnesia descend so quickly."[30] In our interview in 2012 she went on to say:

> I am shocked, I am horrified. I understand that people were chagrined and upset that our regulators turned out to be so weak and feeble. But you do not turn feeble regulators into strong regulators by cutting their budget year after year. Deregulations are still not completed. And I don't understand it. Typically, that's

the kind of thing that comes when the collateral damage is healed and things are all back to normal; but we still have unbelievable foreclosure rates. We still have interest rates that are so low, you can't make any money on it on your savings.

A mere eight years after the fall of Lehman Brothers, complete "amnesia" had set in. The 2016 Republican Party platform rather breathtakingly cited as the *only* cause of the breakdown (in spite of all evidence to the contrary) "the government's own housing policies" and blamed the Dodd-Frank Act and "bureaucracies" for "creating more risks."[31] Donald Trump went so far as to propose a moratorium on financial regulations entirely.[32] Regulation was the disease, not the cure. The centrality of deregulation of banking laws—vertical integration,[33] the availability of risky investment instruments, massively leveraged loans—and the widespread white-collar crime that was spawned from this movement were completely deleted from this painful assessment of the crisis.[34] Criminologist Henry Pontell has pointed out that this is hardly new. For other financial disasters, like the savings and loan crisis, there have been previous attempts to "whitewash white collar crime" by minimizing the role of fraud and criminal actions only to let them "serve as virtual blueprints for future financial disasters."[35] History was repeating itself.

The theme of amnesia and how little had changed since Madoff arose multiple times in my conversations with the UK and US journalists when I asked them to reflect on reportage about white-collar crime following the crisis and the Madoff period. They concurred that overall the conversation about white-collar crime had not shifted significantly. Alex Berenson of the *New York Times* when asked, "Since you originally wrote about the Madoff case, have you noticed a change in the coverage of financial crime?" noted:

> Has there been any *real* change in coverage? No. After Enron and Tyco, in general there was a lot more skepticism towards CEOs and even more skepticism towards corporate accounting. Whereas this hasn't really driven any major changes in coverage or telling.

Christina Boyle of the *Daily News* agreed:

> Did it change coverage of white-collar crimes? Not that I'm aware of . . . *I feel like it's a stand-alone case* . . . I think now you can use just "Madoff" and everyone all

the sudden understands what that means. You don't need to go into the whole background. So for a tabloid it's basically an easy way to just go, "Oh, it's a mini Madoff," like a "mini 9/11."

Tomoeh Murakami Tse of the *Washington Post* similarly described the almost cosmetic changes to journalism, where the name "Madoff" became easily recognizable shorthand:

> I don't think [the Madoff case had an impact on reportage of financial crime]. It didn't fundamentally change the way white-collar crime is covered, [just] certain things like the words [used] . . . People who were [involved in] Ponzi schemes or scandals, they're called "mini Madoffs" . . . And then you'll still see phrases today like "the biggest scandal since the Madoff scandal."

A few of the journalists attributed this lack of evolution in reportage to the cyclical nature of economic crises and the business cycle: when the immediacy of the crises is over and normalcy returns, it is easy to be lulled into complacency, to believe all is behind, to return to the "devil you know." James Doran of the *Guardian*, London *Times*, and *New York Post* described:

> I don't think [the coverage of financial crime] has changed as much as it should have done . . . I've been a business journalist for twenty years. The economy and finance and business is cyclical in every respect, and also for frauds and crime, these things happen time and time again . . . Business is a curious thing. When people are making money they don't care. William Cobbett was quoted as saying, "I defy you to agitate a fellow with a full stomach." When they are making money they don't care how it's coming to them.

James Bone of the London *Times* remarked, almost identically to Doran: "Periodically with the business cycle, people feel that something's wrong with the system. Then the system starts doing well again, and people forget about it."

Ironically, the "stand-alone" quality of the Madoff name may have set the bar too high for other white-collar crimes to enter the headlines, especially in tabloids with limited coverage of business and finance. In other words, because the crime was so massive, so sensational, and affected so many, other instances of white-collar wrongdoing were perceived as unable to attract the same amount of attention. Subsequently, they often went ignored and unreported. Kaja Whitehouse of the *New York Post* remarked, "There were so many scams that emerged that we didn't have time for them, and nobody cared, because Bernie Madoff was just dwarfing everything."

John Marzulli told me an anecdote of how in 2011, "after Madoff," he couldn't interest his editor in the story of a Staten Island Ponzi scheme artist, Joseph Mazella. When asked about his perception of the editor's unwillingness to run the story, he replied:

> We were talking about *Bernie Madoff*, a case with implications felt all over the world, [so how do you compare that with] some clown from Staten Island? That case was maybe fourteen million. It's a Ponzi case in the seven figures—I don't even think they would pay attention to it at this point . . . *There's no case like Madoff.*

Looking Up the Ladder and verstehen: *Roles for Journalists and Scholars*

"There's no case like Madoff." In a way, Marzulli's statement provides a fitting introduction for a final discussion that does not simply lament the futility of all action in the face of trenchant ideology and social resistance to systemic change. Criminologist Jock Young warned against thought that would conclude, "There's no case like Madoff," and against taking Madoff as a pathological aberration rather than the organic product of the socioeconomic order. "The principal biographies so far of Bernie Madoff . . . wonder what made him tick, as if there were some mysterious elements of malice and deceit residing within his personality. In fact, he was perfectly normal. What made him tick was finance capital in the twenty-first century."[36] Young would write elsewhere, "We usually spend our time looking down, not up, the social structure when analyzing criminal behavior."[37] Yet the Madoff case proved eyes can be raised "up." Michael Levi in his "Social Reactions to White-collar Crimes and Their Relationship to Economic Crises" remarks, "Sometimes, moral outrage following dramatic events leads to legislation being passed that has a significant potential effect on corporate elites."[38] There is a very rich possibility for financial crimes to become conduits to engage a broad audience and through which to discuss, to increase civic participation and inspire protest, to address and take action on a wide range of economic and social issues.

Journalists and scholars have a more active role to play in "looking up" to the wrongdoing of the elite. They can provide the mainstream with a deeper, more lucid understanding of financial crimes and their structural underpinnings. Questions to be addressed include, How does the Ponzi culture produced by casino capitalism affect not only the poor but also the middle class and affluent? What commonalities can be found that speak to a similar etiology for street crimes and crimes of the elite (for instance, in the types of strains experienced by the demands for infinite accumulation and materialistic success at all costs)? Can anything short of revolution transform this reality? How does corporate ownership of media conglomerates affect reportage on financial crime? What is the relationship of normative attitudes and discourse to punitive policies and sentencing of financial crime? How do historical and economic phenomena like the booms and busts of the business cycle change those discourses and affect policy? At what point does a white-collar offense become "newsworthy"? How can white-collar crime be *made* newsworthy?

One facet of providing the public with understanding is through more qualitative research that humanizes offenders. Cultural criminologists have urged (although not explicitly for financial, white-collar offenders) researchers to seek *verstehen* in the course of their work, an important sociological term used in this instance to describe a "subjective appreciation and empathic understanding of crime's situated meanings, symbolism, and emotions."[39] Such an approach can remove the urge to immediately assign to financial offenders the "bad apple" label, and find both continuities and breaks with the subjective understandings, motivations, and emotions of other criminal actors and among citizens who have not been branded "criminal" but who nevertheless have been steeped in Ponzis, money, and neoliberal culture.

The act of using empathy as a theoretical tool, of seeking subjective interpretations of crime from the offenders themselves, carries with it of course the risk of appearing sympathetic, of taking offenders at their word, of ignoring the severity of the crime committed, or of privileging the offender's experience over that of the victim. These are certainly criticisms that must be carefully considered, as I have learned intimately in the journey of writing this book. Yet without inquiring into the actual construction of events given by the offender, attempts to deter or influence these crimes will be based purely on speculation. With the case of Bernie Madoff, other than a general pronouncement of his moral turpitude and greed, the media largely left the question of why he committed the crime unasked. Madoff would remark to me:

> I find it interesting that there was little, if any, coverage of . . . "Why did Bernie do this?" . . . I do realize that I chose not to go public to any great extent with the explanation at the time. That being said, it seemed that everyone, including the media, would rather ignore this subject and stick with the MONSTER theory of Bernie just being a crook . . . They chose to do this even though it made no sense.

Madoff's trenchant self-observation is confirmed by others with a more extensive understanding of the patterns of study and discussion within sociology and criminology. The only social scientist to ask seriously why he committed his crime was Jock Young. And in her recent review of white-collar crime, Sally Simpson writes, "[There is] limited empirical evidence at the individual offender level." Continued resistance to making white-collar criminals the subject of expansive inquiry has meant we know almost nothing of Madoff's—and white-collar criminals'—self-described motives to this day.

Other than Jock Young's, one of the sole attempts to understand the subjective experience of Bernie Madoff came not from academia or the media, but from an artist, Deborah Margolin. In this sense, inspiration to provide criminological *verstehen* might be found in her work. Margolin, an OBIE-award-winning playwright who teaches theater studies at Yale University, at first faced stern criticism and legal intimidations for her play *Imagining Madoff*, its first run in 2010 occurring a year after his conviction. The original script revolved around a fantastical conversation between a fictionalized Bernie Madoff and Elie Wiesel, the Nobel Peace laureate and Holocaust survivor who had lost not only his own wealth but his charity's through the fraud. Wiesel, declaring the play "defamatory" and "obscene," threatened to alert his attorney to shut down the play anywhere it might try to open.[40] Margolin removed the Wiesel character, replacing him with the strikingly similar yet completely fictional character of Solomon Galkin, a poet and Holocaust survivor.

In the revised script, Madoff, now in prison, recalls an all-night discussion he had with Galkin in his study, a dialogue on which most of the play centers as the two banter, weaving discussions of love, money, religion, and death. Margolin, who made no claims to verisimilitude, would give her fictional Madoff a strong, reflective voice, one that feels emotion and is even poetic. "It's painful to be able to lie as easily as I'm able to lie," the character laments. "It's like writing a story or singing a song, I just tell the truth in a completely false way. Like changing the color of something that's already there. It makes me sad, to be able to lie so easily." Margolin's Madoff would also attempt to describe his motive for the Ponzi: "I didn't really care that much about the money. I want people to know that. I did it because of the movement, somehow. There was the *music* of it. Moving, moving, and moving. In movements. The money. It was hard, when we were kids. I saw how hard it was. There wasn't much, and you had to move fast. The money moved fast, it was under the surface, hard to see, like salmon spawning, I always thought of fish. I thought of people trying to catch fish . . . I just wanted to grab one." *Imagining Madoff* hinted at the psychological drives of Madoff and at biographical incidents which would presage his engagement in the Ponzi, but it also raised questions of the accountability and motives of other characters and the role of faith, on multiple levels—for instance, the faith of investors like the fictional Galkin who placed their trust in Madoff implicitly. Margolin's Madoff at first resists Galkin's attempts to take his personal money for investment and is on the verge of telling him about the scheme, but Galkin will not listen.

The play would go on to earn positive reviews from the *Washington Post, Tampa Bay Times, St. Louis Post-Dispatch*, and the *Boston Globe*. In keeping with the US media's characteristic presentation of Madoff, the *Globe* would title the review "*Imagining Madoff* Gives the Face of Evil a Voice."[41] In our interview, I asked Margolin to comment on why she chose to "listen" for Madoff's voice when writing her play, why she included his point of view. She responded:

> We ignore the humanity of such criminals at our peril . . . When it's all said and done, he's just some guy . . . like the [Germanwings pilot] who crashed the plane into the French Alps . . . Look at the forensic work that's being done to try to figure out what was going on in the mind of [that man[42]] . . . We need to think about [Madoff]. He's not the devil. There is this desire to mythologize angels and devils. When all is said and done, they're just folks. He's just an asshole with psychological problems. We sequester him from our own humanity at our peril. Why shouldn't we consider the human struggle of a man like this? We have to.

Margolin strongly articulates the need for criminological *verstehen*, and through the play has provided an artistic rendition of this understanding. Through my interviews with Madoff, I attempt to provide an example of how this might look for future research by examining his narratives about why he committed his crime. One does not have to believe in the veracity of his story's details to begin to hear significant themes emerge that speak to the structural, systemic influences that must be considered if we are to go beyond individual, "bad apple" explanations for financial crime in the neoliberal period.

The Banality of Risk

The most prominent recurring theme in the Madoff narratives I will present centers on what, in a turn on Hannah Arendt's phrase "the banality of evil,"[43] I will term the "banality of risk," by which I mean the normalization of taking potentially destabilizing and devastating amounts of risk under pressure for profit. Kathleen Tierney's *Social Roots of Risk: Producing Disasters, Promoting Resilience* argues that disasters like the crisis of 2008 and their impacts are socially produced, and therefore resilience to future disasters can also be socially manufactured.[44] This is clearly exemplified in the way the level of financial risk has been allowed to rise dramatically over the past thirty to forty years in global markets. Opaque products have become riskier and the potential for losses has grown dramatically. Lightning-fast trades made by high-frequency trading firms relying on complicated computer algorithms raise concerns for regulators around the world.[45]

As the structure of markets has facilitated the greater taking of risk, there comes the tantalizing possibility of achieving greater rewards quickly, however unequally they may be distributed. Within the past decade pioneering research by John Coates, a neuroscientist and former derivatives trader for Goldman Sachs, has shown that judgment-impairing physiological and neurological reactions come with this strategic, profit-oriented marketplace gambling. Intense, narcotic-like effects follow successful risk taking, thus leading to more risking taking and upping the ante. In a statement almost tailor-made for a description of Madoff, Coates writes, "An above-average win or loss in the markets, or an ongoing series of wins or losses, can change us, Jekyll-and-Hyde-like, beyond all recognition."[46]

The influence of these systemic factors on the behavior of those who, like Madoff, are embedded in the logic of the markets deserves consideration. In the neoliberal era, those who take on risk (at least in financial and business matters) are often presented as pioneering and gutsy—it is the risk takers who are the innovators, who are willing to put everything on the line to achieve their entrepreneurial visions and reach the American Dream. The less copacetic consequences are brushed aside until a moment of crisis brings them to attention.

Bernie Madoff, reflecting on his crime and often raising rhetorical questions about why and how he had engaged in the massive Ponzi, frequently pointed out to me the enormous risks taken in the course of legitimate business, which has the gradual effect, almost as with alcohol or drugs, of producing a "tolerance" to risk, of habituating one to the uncertainties or reservations that one might expect to intervene in the decision-making process. But more than this, these risks take place in a milieu that rewards and encourages those who take risk, as long as they continue, of course, to be successful:

> It is painful knowing the suffering I caused to people who had trusted me, the devastation I caused my family and the knowledge that I caused the death of my son . . . Every attorney and other visitor has told me that there must have

been some other explanation that caused me to go off the tracks. I know all about COMPARMENTALIZATION and DENIAL but I still can't accept this . . . Unfortunately the culture of Wall Street and the very nature of being a market maker that requires risking huge sums on a daily basis, and had been successful doing so, has played a role that few understand.

He expanded on the integral relationship between risk and Wall Street, suggesting it as almost a kind of "gateway" drug or crime, leading down the rabbit hole to sometimes enormous frauds:

Wall Street is RISK business. This does not in any way mean that I am trying to excuse my wrong doing . . . In the area that I specialized in, Market Making and Proprietary Trading, we were always not only expected to take risks, we were REQUIRED to take some risks in maintaining orderly markets. Basically there would be no possibility of profits to us or our clients had we failed to take some risk daily. A good example is market makers trading from the short side at times and therefore subjecting themselves to losses. In my case I lived with this constantly.

Madoff's suggestion that there are social influences that affect financial risk taking (which in turn impacts the ease with which one might enter into a fraud) is not without its empirical support based on limited studies. Only in the past few decades have scholars become more interested in "financial risk tolerance," expanding upon an overwhelming amount of research about nonfinancial risk tolerance, say for substance abuse. There is evidence based on this research that financial risk tolerance is affected by a combination of environmental/ demographic[47] and psychological factors. For example, individuals with Type A personalities (competitive, aggressive, impatient) or those who score high on sensation-seeking personality dimensions are predictably more likely to engage in financial risk-taking behaviors than those with Type B personalities. Women have been shown to be more financially risk-averse than men,[48] as are blacks and Hispanics compared to whites, whereas level of education positively corresponds to greater risk tolerance.[49] Here one can see an invitation for scholars from the social sciences to fruitfully extend their work. In what ways have systemic changes in risk levels (in regulation, capital reserve requirements, the proliferation of derivatives, socializing risk and privatizing gain, the relentless drive to show "growth" in every quarter), where risk taking and manipulation of loopholes are encouraged, provided the ideal incubator for tolerance and lack of deep ethical concern?

The banality of risk dovetails with two additional themes found in Madoff's explanation of events, which convey a deeper understanding of the crime: the expectation of wealthy investors for large, favorable returns, *always*, in spite of the vicissitudes of the markets; and the ability to view himself and others who commit crime as essentially non-criminal, as people who just went off track unintentionally and lost their way—people who made mistakes or errors in judgment. These themes reveal how Madoff had manufactured for himself a reality where fraud is acceptable and even justified.

In a handwritten letter from prison, Madoff described how in the early 1980s, in the lead-up to the Ponzi, his biggest American clients in his clandestine investment advisory business were asking him to devise a strategy that would allow them to avoid what they considered to be high taxes on short-term trading gains. Prior to this period, Madoff reported that he had invested their money in a strategy known as convertible arbitrage, making for these clients large profits of up to 20 percent. With the new strategy, Madoff invested their money in "a diversified basket of equities with the potential of achieving long term gains . . . that would be taxed at the lower rate." Warning his clients that unlike his previous strategy the new one entailed more risk, Madoff says he also tried to limit this by hedging the long positions with short sales. Although he did not give specific dates, Madoff said that over time, with changes made by the IRS, he revised this model several times to devise more "exotic" and risky hedges that continued to help these clients avoid high taxes. Simultaneously, several of his large European clients in France were trying to find ways of dodging the payment of high taxes and also get their money into US dollars in the wake of the election of socialist François Mitterrand in 1981. These clients provided the perfect counterparties, therefore, to his US clients' trades.

"Everything went fine for years," he said, until the 1987 crash. His US investors became skittish at the thought that their long-term profits might disappear, and forced Madoff to sell their positions in violation of the agreement with the European investors and Madoff. "In order to avoid lengthy and ugly litigation of the default, that would hurt the reputation of everyone," he took on their hedge positions, but asked that they agree to assume any losses he might incur. They did agree, but as the market began to recover, "[their] greed began to get the upper hand and in order to protect their potential commitment to cover my losses . . . they started to make outside investments" which were performing poorly. Again he revised his investment strategy with these clients, "to increase [his] profits and also replace the capital I was using to cover the hedge losses that were starting to build," to a "basket of 35 equities hedged with index options on the S&P 100"—the now infamous "split strike" strategy.[50] "More monies started to flow in as word got out that Bernie had a new strategy for hedge funds and high net worth clients," he wrote.

Madoff claimed that in spite of the stickiness of the situation in which he found himself in the 1987 crash, the Ponzi did not begin then but rather at the start of the Gulf War and the economic recession of the early 1990s. He was stuck "sit[ting] with [his clients' money] in U.S. Treasuries waiting for the market to become receptive," rather than executing the split strike strategy.

> This led to the funds pressing me to get into the market to trade, as well as the high net worth clients also growing impatient . . . I foolishly convinced myself that I should short the strategy to the clients losing the spread between the yield on the treasuries and the expected spread on a successful [split strike conversion] trade . . . The rest is my tragic history of never being able to recover.

In his public statement before Judge Chin, Madoff additionally noted: "I felt compelled to satisfy my clients' expectations, at any cost . . . I therefore claimed that I employed an investment strategy I had developed, called the split strike conversion strategy, to falsely give the appearance to clients that I had achieved the results I believed they expected."

In analyzing Madoff's narration of the events leading up to the Ponzi—regardless of the veracity of the timeline, which has been extensively contested—one notices the emphasis he placed on the pressure he felt to live up to the expectations of his "greedy," impatient investors, whose faith in him and loyalty was premised on his ability to be a market wizard, to outperform and achieve high returns even in a down market. Some scholars of financial crime have described this motivation for engaging in wrongdoing a "fear of falling." Such white-collar offenders, they state, would be "reasonably happy with the place they have achieved through conventional means if only they could keep that place. But the fate of organizational success and failure, or the changing nature of the economy in their line of work, may put them at least temporarily under great financial pressure . . . They may perceive this situation as a short-term threat that can be met through short-term fraud—a temporary taking to be restored as soon as business fortunes turn around."[51] The motive here is not pecuniary gain per se but an avoidance of losing what has *already* been gained, not only monetarily but also in prestige and reputation. Madoff's explanation of the events leading up to the Ponzi is remarkably in agreement with this theory, and also reflects a recurrent theme in his narrative that he was otherwise a good person, that this was simply a "mistake." In a letter to me about the crime, he wrote:

> When I began my tragic mistake of going short on the Split Strike strategy with my clients I felt it was a reasonable TEMPORARY trade until the markets became liquid enough to fulfill my original commitments to my clients . . . I became trapped into a never-ending spiral of risk. I can assure you that the London Whale trader at JP Morgan had not expected to lose 6 billion dollars in his trading strategy . . . I could give you an endless list of examples such as this where most of these individuals were basically honest . . . who became involved in similar problems.

He made a similar claim before Judge Chin prior to his sentencing:

> When I began the Ponzi scheme I believed it would end shortly and I would be able to extricate myself and my clients from the scheme. However, this proved difficult, and ultimately impossible, and as the years went by I realized that my arrest and this day would inevitably come.

In my interview with Diana Henriques, the *New York Times* journalist and one of the few reporters given prison access to Madoff for her book *Wizard of Lies: Bernie Madoff and the Death of Trust*, she reflected on what she believed led Madoff to his crime:

> His legitimate story—the "Dr. Jekyll" story—was a legitimate success story. Yet, behind it was this darker story, where I think Madoff's insatiable appetite for praise and admiration led him to become a criminal. Managing money was the only thing he ever tried to do that he wasn't successful at . . . He could not admit failure at anything. He found it much easier to live with himself as a liar than to live with himself as a failure. So to the extent that the pursuit of the American Dream is implicated in the Madoff story, it is in his own personal inability to admit that he had failed. We deify the pursuit of the American Dream to such an extent that to fail to achieve it has such psychic consequences for those who fail; that I think in his case, he couldn't endure them. He couldn't admit that he couldn't live up to the outlandish admiration that he was generating.

Stephen Foley offered a comparable analysis:

> I think a large number of frauds that are generally attributed to greed are actually more likely to begin out of fear . . . Fear of having made a mistake and being discovered. Fear of having to own up to something. Fear of people who think that you're one thing discovering that you're another type or not as successful as you actually are. I think a lot of frauds begin by people covering up a mistake. To the extent that I would, you know, write a fictionalized account of Madoff's life, it would probably begin with two or three months' worth of poor investment returns that he then faked.

If we are to believe Madoff's written testimony of his crime, Foley's "fictional account" would be indeed accurate. Here Henriques and Foley go beyond the "bad apple" approach which was so characteristic of the public response, not only to Madoff but to the SEC for its regulatory failures, and even to the "1%" as a group. Henriques points out that the inability of Madoff to accept failure was deeply informed by a cultural, individualistic ethos that will not permit losing, which designates failure as an internal flaw, not the product of circumstance. To understand the impact of this cultural imperative is not to excuse the criminal behavior that results, but it helps us explain its origins, just as sociologists have tried for over a century to understand "street" crimes in terms of primarily economic strain. The additional themes found in Madoff's own narrative, of risk taking and pressure from investors whose drive for profit denied the limitations of a volatile market, can form the beginning of a criminological *verstehen* of his crime, one that goes beyond labeling Madoff as "evil" or "the Devil." Instead, we begin to arrive at an understanding of the way capitalism in the neoliberal period sets the stage for such crimes at the same time that it sets the stage for financial crisis. The two are intertwined.

Toward a News-making Criminology

I do not here offer any prescriptions for new regulation or fixed regulation, nor do I offer policy recommendations. Pontell, Geis, Reichman, and other criminologists have already done so in response to Madoff.[52] To do so would deny what I think to be one of the crucial insights this book offers: that until a much deeper cultural and ideological shift happens, any "on paper" changes will be just as easily swept aside as Harry Markopolos's numerous warnings to the SEC. How to achieve such a shift is well beyond the scope of this analysis and would involve social movements, politicians, and educators, but I argue that there is a direct, large role for journalists, and scholars and educators (from the social sciences and beyond), in this endeavor.

One challenge for these groups is how to make white-collar crime understandable and relevant to the public during all phases of the business cycle. There is, for a multitude of reasons, a traditional lack of public attention to financial wrongdoing *unless* there is either a major crisis, a gargantuan individual case of fraud of Madoff-like proportions, or a combination of these two. Unfortunately, as my interviews with journalists indicate, after Madoff and the financial crisis there was little movement to reposition financial crime either in the media or, I would add, in academia as a topic to be pursued with the same zeal as street crimes. Attention to white-collar fraud fluctuates and is forgotten in times of relative economic prosperity or at least under the *illusion* of prosperity for all. But journalists, scholars, and politicians, those who have the ability to shape public discourse, are not without agency in the process. James Doran commented insightfully:

> I don't think enough attention is being put on financial crime. I don't think newspapers take it as seriously as they ought . . . It's a very complicated business, fraud. Or it *seems* to be a complicated business; it's actually all very simple. We haven't done enough to demystify financial crime and that's a sin, because people will continue to be sucked in.

As Doran implies, there is a *perception* of the inscrutability of fraud and corporate crime for a general readership. This is not to deny that explaining the rigging of LIBOR, for example, is not inherently a more complicated project than, say, explaining a run-of-the-mill violent crime of passion—but this makes the "translation" of fraud all the more essential. In "Preemption vs. Punishment: A Comparative Study of White Collar Crime Prosecution in the United States and the United Kingdom," a related analysis and demand is presented: "What the mass media brings to the war against white-collar crime is transparency, the dissemination of knowledge to the public. In doing so, the media plays a part in prevention [and it] has the power to draw national significance to any situation. Their traditional role as public watchdog needs to broaden into a more assertive public spotlight drawing . . . attention to potentially damaging corporate scandals and calling for action. By reporting in detail and frequently about certain corporation actions, the public will scrutinize the corporation's actions and perhaps prevent catastrophic damages by stopping corporate crime at its early stage."[53]

Although sociology and criminology have produced rich studies on the topic of white-collar crime, just as these crimes are downplayed by the mainstream media so too do they occupy a marginalized status within studies of crime. Proof of their conjectures can be found in the top ten criminology and criminal justice journals ranked by prestige. A meager 3.4 percent of all published articles between 2001 and 2009 were white-collar-crime articles.[54] Noted criminologist Gregg Barak has lamented: "Crime reports and research on white-collar crime, pretty much of any kind, are woefully inadequate at best or non-existent at worst. Where they minimally exist, they are typically one-sided in nature, focusing on the attacks against corporations and their interests, and virtually indifferent to the harms and injuries perpetrated by corporations against workers, consumers, taxpayers, and the environment."[55]

In times of economic boom, when fraud receives less attention, it might indeed be difficult to attract attention to white-collar crime. But there are reasons to think that now is a time when public attention could be readily focused upon elite financial malfeasance. The crisis of 2007–9, the subsequent Great Recession, international Occupy movements, and of course Bernie Madoff himself linger in our cultural memory. It is a moment for social scientists to actively commit to exploring intensively white-collar crime, its deep structural and systemic roots, and to bring that to the center. Findings should then be brought outside of the rarefied atmosphere of the ivory tower.

The dearth of research into white-collar crime is sometimes attributed to methodological difficulties and the demands of positivistic inquiry. It may be true that "the field of white-collar crime . . . is particularly resistant to experimental work."[56] There are practical reasons for this lack of study, but solutions should also be devised to help fill in our lack of knowledge in many instances. One hurdle to quantitative assessments is that reliable, basic statistics about white-collar crime are not as readily available as those dealing with street crime due to myriad issues.[57] In the United States, the Department of Justice lacks a national database for white-collar crime statistics. The FBI's Uniform Crime Reports (UCR), the US gold standard for crime statistics, is likewise insufficient for researchers,[58] as it lumps together many types of primarily individual-level white-collar crime under four categories: forgery and counterfeiting, fraud, embezzlement, and all other crimes. And because the UCR does not list white-collar offenses as one of the eight "index" (i.e., serious) offenses, there is limited reportage on these crimes in the media.[59] Adding to this challenge, organizations other than the police are involved with the apprehension, litigation, and prosecution of white-collar crime. In the absence of police records, which comprise a rich source of statistical information, researchers are made dependent on loosely linked (or

unlinked) agencies for their data, which might also be made less readily available. "There is no truly reliable way to measure the incidence
of the many diverse forms of white collar crime, from antitrust violations to violations of environmental law to Medicaid fraud to employee
embezzlement," white-collar crime scholar David Friedrichs writes.[60]
In the United Kingdom one finds similar problems. The Crime Survey
for England and Wales (CSEW) did not include fraud and cybercrime
in their headline estimates until 2016,[61] and data on white-collar crime
must be culled and triangulated from different sources such as police
reports, Action Fraud (the UK's national fraud and cybercrime reporting center), the CSEW, and the National Fraud Intelligence Bureau. The
National Statistician's Crime Statistics for England and Wales states that
"fraud [is] one of the most important gaps in crime statistics."[62]

Another very valid reason for difficulty in performing contemporary research is the inability of social scientists to gain access to persons possessing greater-than-average power, resources, and education
for the purpose of interviews, questionnaires, ethnographies, and the
like. In the United Kingdom, defamation is also a threat. Yet there is no
literature to suggest that any number of failed attempts have even been
made. "Unfortunately, there are far too many criminologists willing to
conduct research on the powerless and far too few willing to conduct
research on the powerful," Barak concludes. As a community of inquiry,
we have to undergo a profound change in reflexivity. Do we continue to
pathologize the poor (and mostly poor persons of color) because they
are convenient subjects of study with comparatively little power to resist
going under the microscope of scientific inquiry?

Balancing our scrutiny by "looking up the ladder" is imperative. To
borrow the language of the Occupy movement, focusing on the crimes of
the "99%" is important work. But I suggest that it is time to begin a "sociology of the 1%" as well, giving more of our attention to elite wrongdoing—
the origins, impacts, structural influences, personality traits, and cultural,
political, economic, and discursive responses. It will empower social
movements and the general populace to identify, understand, and therefore resist the conditions that enable such fraud, and help them realize

the difficult ideological struggles they must wage against "deep faith" in capitalism. It will educate and demystify. As journalist James Doran noted earlier in regard to journalists, it is *because* financial crime can appear abstruse and complex, especially to the general public, that it is even more imperative after a crisis for social scientists to analyze and present research which makes these crimes transparent and cuts through the technicalities to explore the more readily understandable social forces at work.

Barak has rightly called for a "newsmaking criminology"—conscious efforts and activities by those who study crime (I would include journalists as well as scholars) to interpret, influence, and shape the representation of "newsworthy" items about crime and justice.[63] Wrongdoing by the powerful, like significant financial crimes but also legal but unethical behavior, has catastrophic consequences. It must be presented *as* a major social problem that creates *actual* harm, which if not literally and directly violent, is metaphorically and indirectly violent. Importantly, this approach must not be reduced to reproducing the same narratives about criminality in the same way "street" criminals have been constructed as "abnormal" and the solution to their crimes presented as "more punishment." The structures of capitalism that undergird these offenses are themselves criminogenic and create "cultures" of risk taking with the livelihoods of others, avarice, commodification, and complete disregard for widening social inequality. They should be exposed as such, and real work should be spent on the creative, disruptive work necessary to make systemic changes.

• • •

As the preceding chapters have shown, media discourses about Madoff's crime have focused on his individual, egregious behavior and the mistakes or ethical lapses of other individuals—modes of analysis that were also extrapolated to the financial crisis of 2008. What was painfully lacking was a positioning and discussion of Madoff's place within the overall culture of modern capitalism and the conditions that led—and will lead again—to economic collapse. In other words, our cultural scripts, embedded in the logic of capitalism, proved ultimately impermeable to change and reproduced themselves through the Madoff case.

Madoff's status as a notorious cultural icon is firmly established. His classically tragic story is now part of our shared knowledge, a parable of greed leading to demise. But in using *verstehen* to contemplate this larger-than-life villain in context, and by analyzing our own responses to his crime, we can see the dangers of, as Margolin said, sequestering him from our humanity. To better our chances of lessening financial crime and improving the system in which it occurs, I hope that we can, and will, move past simplistic descriptions of financial criminals as metaphysically "evil," descriptions which make offenders like Bernie Madoff accountable for the pernicious structural problems with free-market capitalism that still have to be overcome.

APPENDIX: INTERVIEWEES*

Anton Antonowicz, US correspondent, *Daily Mirror*

Binyamin Appelbaum, staff writer, *Washington Post*, and currently Washington correspondent, *New York Times*

Erin Arvedlund, financial journalist, TheStreet.com, *Barron's*, *Wall Street Journal*, *New York Times*, *Moscow Times*, and Porfolio.com, and author of *Too Good to Be True: The Rise and Fall of Bernie Madoff*

Alex Berenson, journalist, *New York Times*, previously at TheStreet.com

James Bone, journalist, London *Times*

Christina Boyle, staff reporter, *New York Daily News*

Andrew Clark, deputy business editor, London *Times*, and previously business editor, the *Observer*; previous work for the *Guardian*, *Daily Telegraph*, *Sunday Business*, and *Sydney Morning Herald*

James Doran, Wall Street bureau chief, London *Times*, and freelance journalist for the *Guardian*, the *Observer*, *New York Metro*, and *New York Post*

Stephen Foley, associate business editor, the *Independent*, based in New York; currently markets correspondent, *Financial Times*

Alexandra Frean, US business correspondent, London *Times*, based in New York

David Gelles, US mergers and acquisitions correspondent, Financial Times, based in New York

Zachary Goldfarb, staff writer, *Washington Post*, covering financial regulation and government investigations into corporate wrongdoing

---

* Affiliations were at the time of the interviews.

Peter Henning, contributor, DealBook (*New York Times*); professor, Wayne State University Law School; and former prosecutor, Justice Department, Security and Exchange Commission enforcement division

Diana Henriques, financial reporter, *New York Times*, and author of *Wizard of Lies: Bernie Madoff and the Death of Trust*

Caitlin Thorne Hersey, freelance photographer, *New York Post*

Serge Kovaleski, national correspondent, *New York Times*

Tom Leonard, US correspondent, *Daily Mail*

Bernard Madoff

Deborah Margolin, Obie-award-winning American playwright and performance artist, and author of *Imagining Madoff*

John Marzulli, federal court reporter, *New York Daily News*

Tomoeh Murakami Tse, financial reporter, *Washington Post*, based in New York

John Nester, chief spokesperson, Securities and Exchange Commission

Ed Pilkington, New York correspondent, the *Guardian*

Gary Silverman, US deputy managing editor, *Financial Times*, previously US news editor

Leslie Wayne, business and finance reporter, *New York Times*

Kaja Whitehouse, business reporter, *New York Post*

Tom Zambito, court reporter, *New York Daily News*

NOTES

Chapter 1

1. A. Zibel, "Fannie, Freddie Loans Deemed 'Safe' under Mortgage Rules," *Wall Street Journal*, March 28, 2011.

2. U.S. Department of the Treasury, "TARP Programs," 2015, www.treasury.gov/initiatives/financial-stability/TARP-Programs/Pages/default.aspx#.

3. U.S. Department of the Treasury, "Asset Guarantee Program," 2013, www.treasury.gov/initiatives/financial-stability/TARP-Programs/bank-investment-programs/agp/Pages/default.aspx.

4. Financial Crisis Inquiry Commission, *Financial Crisis Inquiry Report* (Washington, DC: U.S. Government Printing Office, 2011), 390–91.

5. "UK Unemployment Climbs to 2.47 M," BBC News, September 16, 2009.

6. D. Henriques, "New Description on Timing of Madoff's Confession," *New York Times*, January 9, 2009.

7. For much more extended treatments of the case from journalistic perspectives without sensationalism, see E. Arvedlund, *Too Good to Be True: The Rise and Fall of Bernie Madoff* (New York: Portfolio, 2009); and D. Henriques, *The Wizard of Lies: Bernie Madoff and the Death of Trust* (New York: St. Martin's Press, 2011).

8. Arvedlund, *Too Good to Be True*.

9. Madoff would later have a seat on the Hofstra board of trustees, even serving as a Gala Dinner Committee member, although Hofstra never invested with him.

10. J. Cresswell and L. Thomas Jr., "The Talented Mr. Madoff," *New York Times*, January 24, 2009.

11. M. de la Merced, "Effort Under Way to Sell Madoff Unit," *New York Times*, December 24, 2009.

12. D. Lieberman, P. Gogoi, T. Howard, K. McCoy, and M. Krantz, "Investors Remain Amazed by Madoff's Sudden Downfall," *USA Today*, December 12, 2008.

13. B. Appelbaum and D. Hilzenrath, "SEC Didn't Act on Madoff Tips," *Washington Post*, December 16, 2008. See also A. Lucchetti, K. Scannel, and Amir Efrati, "SEC to Probe Its Ties to Madoffs," *Wall Street Journal*, December 17, 2008.

14. Henriques, *Wizard of Lies*, 96; and Arvedlund, *Too Good to Be True*, 26–27.

15. Several of his long-standing clients, including businessman Jeffrey Picower, had Madoff accounts with annual rates of return of up to 950 percent. See C. L. Lewis, "How Madoff Did It: Victims' Accounts," *Society* 48 (2011): 70–76.

16. Transcript of United States of America v. Bernard L. Madoff, filed as Case No. 09-cr-213 in U.S. District Court, New York, March 12, 2009.

17. Z. Kouwe, "A Look at Madoff Trading Records," *New York Times*, December 15, 2008.

18. A. Berenson, "Even Winners May Lose with Madoff," *New York Times*, December 18, 2008.

19. D. Henry and E. Flitter, "Decades-long Ties to Madoff Cost JP Morgan 2.6 Billion," Reuters, January 7, 2014. See also H. D. Chaitman and L. Gotthoffer's independently published *JP Madoff* (2015), which is an excoriating indictment of J. P. Morgan, going into great detail of the bank's alleged knowledge of Madoff and other improprieties such as the London Whale incident.

20. Former SEC chairman Harvey Pitt is quoted as saying, "There's no question the amounts are probably north of $10 billion," but indicated they were probably under the $17 billion estimated by the Madoff trustee. See S. Shamir, "Extent of Madoff Fraud Now Estimated at Far Below $50b," *Haaretz*, August 3, 2009.

21. K. McCoy, "Estimate of Madoff Victims Grows," *USA Today*, May 14, 2014.

22. B. Ross, *The Madoff Chronicles: Inside the Secret World of Bernie and Ruth* (New York: Hyperion, 2009), 31.

23. "Manhattan U.S. Attorney Files Additional Charges against Former Employees of Bernard L. Madoff Securities LLC" (press release), Federal Bureau of Investigation, October 1, 2012, www.fbi.gov/newyork/press-releases/2012/manhattan-u.s.-attorney -files-additional-charges-against-former-employees-of-bernard-l.-madoff-investment- securities-llc.

24. Madoff, personal correspondence.

25. *Discourse* has been defined as "the particular ways of talking about and understanding aspects of the world" by M. Jorgensen and L. Phillips in *Discourse Analysis as Theory and Method* (Thousand Oaks, CA: Sage, 2002). At its most basic level, discourse analysis—a method on which this book relies—is the study of language in use (see J. P. Gee, *An Introduction to Discourse Analysis: Theory and Method* [New York: Routledge, 1999]). In a statement that relates importantly to this book, Gee wrote in a blog post: "Our job, as discourse analysts, is not to judge . . . and not to reach definitive truths. Our job is to deepen the conversations among frameworks." See Gee, "The Importance of Discourse Analysis," http://mo.jamespaulgee.com/moessaydisp .php?id=193&scateg=Linguistics, accessed August 25, 2016.

26. D. M. Kotz, "Globalization and Neoliberalism," *Rethinking Marxism* 12 (2002): 64–79, offers a good summary of neoliberalism's key ingredients. As an ideology, neoliberalism saw rapid expansion in the 1970s. Among its precepts it holds that laissez-faire, minimally regulated free-market capitalism will swiftly, efficiently, and effectively maximize economic growth and lead to rapid social and technological progress. The role of the state, therefore, should be curtailed and noninterventionist, both in terms of its regulation of business and its provision of social programs and benefits. At the international level, capital, goods, and services should be allowed to flow freely without regard to traditional state boundaries or interference from governments.

27. Social science has long accepted content analysis as a key tool in deciphering social meaning, although over the past one hundred years it has seen variegated definitions. Lasswell, one of its early developers, writes, "Content analysis operates on the view that verbal behavior is a form of human behavior, that the flow of symbols is part of the flow of events, and that the communication process is part of the historical process" (quoted in K. Neuendorf, *The Content Analysis Guidebook* [Thousand Oaks, CA: Sage, 2002]). Krippendorf's seminal text on the subject presents content analysis as a "research technique for making replicable and valid inferences from text . . . Texts have meaning relative to particular contexts, discourses, or purposes" (K. Krippendorf, *Content Analysis: An Introduction to Its Methodology* [Thousand Oaks, CA: Sage, 2004], 18).

28. S. Will, "America's Ponzi Culture," in *How They Got Away With It: White Collar Criminals and the Financial Meltdown*, ed. S. Will, S. Handelman, and D. Brotherton (New York: Columbia University Press, 2013), 48.

29. D. Friedrichs, "Enron et al: Paradigmatic White Collar Crime Cases for the New Century," *Critical Criminology* 12 (2004): 113–32.

30. See K. Calavita, R. Tillman, and H. Pontell, "The Savings and Loan Debacle, Financial Crime, and the State," *Annual Review of Sociology* 23 (1997): 19–38; and the authors' *Big Money Crime: Fraud and Politics in the Savings and Loan Scandal* (Berkeley: University of California Press, 1999) for a more extended treatment.

31. P. Grabosky and N. Shover, "Forestalling the Next Epidemic of White-collar Crime," *Criminology and Public Policy* 9 (2010): 641–54.

32. Will, Handelman, and Brotherton, *How They Got Away With It*.

33. J. Reiman, *The Rich Get Richer and the Poor Get Prison: Ideology, Class, and Criminal Justice* (Boston: Allyn & Bacon, 2001).

34. L. Snider, "The Sociology of Corporate Crime: An Obituary," *Theoretical Criminology* 4 (2000): 169–206. See also Snider, "The Regulatory Dance: Understanding Reform Processes in Corporate Crime," *International Journal of the Sociology of Law* 19 (1991): 209–36.

35. H. Pontell, "White-collar Crime or Just Risky Business? The Role of Fraud in Major Financial Debacle," *Crime, Law and Social Change* 42 (2004): 309–24.

36. N. Fligstein and A. Roehrkasse, "The Causes of Fraud in Financial Crises: Evidence from the Mortgage-Backed Securities Industry," 2015, http://sociology.berkeley.edu/sites/default/files/faculty/fligstein/The%20Causes%20of%20Fraud%20in%20Financial%20Crises%20October%202015.pdf.

37. For example, see E. Sutherland, *White Collar Crime* (New York: Dryden Press, 1949); and Reiman, *Rich Get Richer*.

38. R. Ericson, P. Baranek, and J. Chan have made this claim in *Representing Order: Crime, Law, and Justice in the Media* (Open University Press, 1991).

39. G. Barak, "Media and Crime," in *The Routledge Handbook of Critical Criminology*, ed. W. Dekeseredy and M. Dragewicz (London: Routledge, 2012), 373–85. See also G. Barak, ed., *Media, Process, and the Social Construction of Crime: Studies in Newsmaking Criminology* (New York: Garland, 2004).

40. J. Katz, "What Makes Crime 'News'?" *Media, Culture, and Society* 9 (1987): 47–75.

41. L. Chancer, *High Profile Crimes: When Legal Cases Become Social Causes* (Chicago: University of Chicago Press, 2005).

42. H. Benedict, *Virgin or Vamp: How the Press Covers Sex Crimes* (Oxford: Oxford University Press, 1992).

43. M. Levi, "The Media Construction of Financial White-collar Crimes and Their Relationship to Economic Crises," *Sociology of Crime, Law and Deviance* 16 (2011): 87–105.

44. E. R. Quinney, "The Study of White Collar Crime: Towards a Reorientation in Theory and Research," *Journal of Criminal Law, Criminology, and Political Science* 55 (1964): 11. All emphasis in book is mine unless indicated.

45. K. Holtfreter, S. van Slyke, J. Bratton, and M. Gertz, "Public Perceptions of White-collar Crime and Punishment," *Journal of Criminal Justice* 36 (2008): 50–60.

46. G. Geis, *White-collar and Corporate Crime* (Upper Saddle River, NJ: Pearson, 2007).

47. Wright et al., "The Social Construction of Corporate Violence: Media Coverage of the Imperial Food Products Fire," *Crime and Delinquency* 41 (1995): 20–36, is one such example.

48. J. W. Williams, "The Lessons of Enron: Media Accounts, Corporate Crimes, and Financial Markets," *Theoretical Criminology* 12 (2008): 471–99.

49. M. Levi, "Social Reactions to White-collar Crimes and Their Relationship to Economic Crises," *Sociology of Crime, Law and Deviance* 16 (2011): 87–105.

50. M. Levi, "The Media Construction of Financial White-collar Crimes," *British Journal of Criminology* 46 (2006): 1037–57. See also his "White-collar, Organized and Cyber Crimes in the Media: Some Contrasts and Similarities," *Crime, Law and Social Change* 49 (2008): 365–77; and "Suite Revenge?" *British Journal of Criminology* 49 (2009): 48–67.

51. J. L. Yang, "Here's an Unlikely Bestseller: A 700-page Book on 21st Century Economics," *Washington Post*, April 22, 2014.

Chapter 2

1. "25 People to Blame for the Crisis," *Time*, February 2009, http://content.time.com/time/specials/packages/article/0,28804,1877351_1877350_1877337,00.html. The *Guardian* had also released its own list, which did not feature Madoff. See J. Finch, "The 25 People Responsible for the Global Financial Crisis," *Guardian*, February 25, 2009.

2. S. E. Bird and R.W. Dardenne, "Rethinking News and Myth as Storytelling," in *The Handbook of Journalism Studies*, ed. K. Wahl-Jorgensen and T. Hanitzsch (New York: Routledge, 2009), 205–17.

3. T. Glasser and J. S. Ettema, "Investigative Journalism and the Legitimation of Moral Order," paper presented at the Annual Meeting of the Association for Education in Journalism and Mass Communication, San Antonio, Texas, August 1–4, 1987, 1–41.

4. Ibid., 34.

5. J. Eisinger, "Why Only One Top Banker Went to Jail for the Financial Crisis," *New York Times*, April 30, 2014.

6. K. Calavita, Henry N. Pontell, Robert H. Tillman, *Big Money Crime* (Berkeley: University of California Press, 1999), 156.

7. Eisinger, "Why Only One Top Banker Went to Jail for the Financial Crisis."

8. Confirmation of the cultural dimension of individualism within the United States and the United Kingdom can be found in one of the most widely cited and extensive studies comparing cultures among nation-states, conducted by psychologist Geert Hofstede. Individualist societies such as the United States and United Kingdom have loose ties between group members, and "everyone is expected to look after him/herself and his/her immediate family." Interestingly, only seven of the seventy-one countries Hofstede studied had individualism as their highest dimension. See Geert Hofstede, "Dimensionalizing Cultures: The Hofstede Model in Context," *Online Readings in Psychology and Culture* 2 (2011); and Hofstede and R. R. McRae, "Personality and Culture Revisited: Linking Traits and Dimensions in Culture," *Cross Cultural Research* 38 (2004): 52–88.

9. "Madoff an Egomaniac," *Times* (London), May 7, 2009.

10. M. Waller, "More on the Bizarre World of Bernie," *Times* (London), June 2, 2009.

11. M. Goslett, "I just can't live with that camera—it's not square; Inside the Bizarre World of £30bn Pyramid Schemester," *Daily Mail*, January 3, 2009.

12. J. Creswell and L. Thomas Jr., "The Talented Mr. Madoff," *New York Times*, January 25, 2009.

13. A. Karni, "Total Headcase," *New York Post*, August 2, 2009.

14. J. Marzulli, "Call Him Ponz Scum," *Daily News* (NY), January 24, 2012.

15. C. Manning and G. Hiscott, "Your Money Heroes and Villains of 2008," *Daily Mirror*, December 30, 2008.

16. R. Blumenthal, "If Bernie Met Dante," *New York Times*, March 15, 2009.

17. M. Kakutan, "A Scoundrel in the Land of the Lax," *New York Times*, August 19, 2009.

18. R. Blumenthal, "If Bernie Met Dante," *New York Times*, March 15, 2009. See also D. Henriques, "Madoff, Apologizing, Is Given 150 Years," *New York Times*, June 30, 2009.

19. F. Rich, "Who Wants to Kick a Millionaire," *New York Times*, December 21, 2008.

20. D. Segal and A. L. Cowan, "The Madoffs Shared Much; Question Is How Much," *New York Times*, January 15, 2009.

21. B. Macintyre, "The Way We Read Now as Our World Totters; Sales of Romantic Fiction, Dickens and Ayn Rand's Paean to Capitalism Are Soaring, but Nothing Beats F. Scott Fitzgerald," *Times* (London), March 12, 2009.

22. C. Seib, "The Madoff I Knew," *The Times* (London), May 7, 2009.

23. "Financial Viewpoint: Madoff, the Midas Who Made an Ass of Investors," *Guardian*, December 16, 2008.

24. M. Tomasky, "Comment and Debate: Welcome to America's Hall of Shame," *Guardian*, December 31, 2008.

25. B. Golding and K. Mokha, "Ezra Pounded by Andy Suit—Blew Clients' $2.4B with Madoff," *New York Post*, April 7, 2009.

26. J. Pressler, "Marc Dreier Is the 'Houdini of Impersonation,'" *New York Magazine*, December 11, 2008.

27. W. Rashbaum, "Bail Is Denied to Lawyer Charged with Huge Fraud," *New York Times*, December 12, 2008.

28. N. Vardi, "Allen Stanford Convicted in $7 Billion Ponzi Scheme," *Forbes*, March 6, 2012. See also B. Golding, "Desperate Lawyer's 'Flight' Is Canceled," *New York Post*, December 12, 2008; and B. Weiser, "Lawyer Gets 20 Years in 700 Million Fraud," *New York Times*, July 13, 2009.

29. K. Zraick, "Man Accused of Running Ponzi Scheme in Brooklyn," *New York Times*, September 9, 2009; and J. Dye, "Philip Barry, 'Brooklyn's Madoff,' Sentenced for Ponzi Scheme," *Huffington Post*, June 17, 2011.

30. "The Cost of the Wall Street-Caused Financial Collapse and Ongoing Economic Crisis Is More than $12.8 Trillion," *Better Markets,* 2012, http://bettermarkets.com/sites/default/files/Cost%20Of%20The%20Crisis_0.pdf.

31. www.madofftrustee.com/.

32. N. Couldry and T. Markham, "Celebrity Culture and Public Connection: Bridge or Chasm?" *International Journal of Cultural Studies* 4 (December 2007): 403–21.

33. M. Levi, "The Media Construction of White Collar Crimes," *British Journal of Criminology* 46 (2006):1037–57.

34. R. Reiner, "Media Made Criminality: Constructions of Crime in the Mass Media," in *The Oxford Handbook of Criminology*, 3rd ed., ed. M. Maguire et al. (Oxford: Oxford University Press, 2007), 302–37.

35. J. MacIntosh, "Even Uma Beau Gets Skimmed," *New York Post*, December 17, 2008.

36. D. Block, "Add Zsa Zsa to Growing List of Big Madoff Victims," *Daily News* (NY), January 25, 2009.

37. S. Young and O. Mortiz, "He's 'Forrest Chump': H'wood Script Writer Sues Investment Mgr. for Losing Big Bucks in Ponzi Scheme," *Daily News* (NY), December 17, 2008.

38. S. Jaggers and C. Seib, "Tremors of Madoff Scandal Spread Wide as Bacon Is Caught Up in the Scandal," *Times* (London), January 1, 2009.

39. E. Smith, "Madoff's !38 Billion Con Ends in Prison," *Sun*, March 13, 2009.

40. P. O'Shaugnessy, "King of Ponzi's Finale: Circus Atmosphere outside Court Belies Sad Fact That There Are Folks Who Lost It All," *Daily News* (NY), June 30, 2009.

41. Associated Press, "Madoff Auction: Jewelry, Luxury Items Fetch High Prices," *Christian Science Monitor*, November 15, 2010.

42. G. E. Newman, G. Giesendruck, and P. Bloom, "Celebrity Contagion and the Value of Objects," *Journal of Consumer Research* (2011): 38.

43. L. Goldberg, "Richard Dreyfuss to Play Bernie Madoff in ABC Drama," *Hollywood Reporter*, February 18, 2015.

44. M. Berkowitz, "The Madoff Paradox: American Jewish Sage, Savior, and Thief," *Journal of American Studies* 46 (2012): 189–202.

45. The national director of the Anti-Defamation League, Abraham Foxman, wrote a bracing discussion of these longstanding stereotypes in the wake of the Madoff scandal. See his *Jews and Money: The Story of a Stereotype* (New York: St. Martin's Press, 2010).

46. D. M. Cohen, "The Jew and Shylock," *Shakespeare Quarterly* 31 (1980): 53–63.

47. L. Lane, "Dickens Archetypal Jew," *PMLA* 73 (1958): 94–100.

48. J. Pascal, "Time to Bury Fagin," *Guardian*, January 17, 2009.

49. See C. Greenberg, "Donald Trump's Conspiracy Theories Sound Anti-Semitic: Does He Even Realize It?" *Washington Post,* October 16, 2006; and H. Chernikoff and N. Guttman, "Donald Trump's Four Jewish Dog Whistles of the Second Presidential Debate," *Haaretz,* October 10, 2016.

50. M. Seal, "Madoff's World," *Vanity Fair*, March 31, 2009.

51. B. Golding and D. Mangan, "Ponzi King Takes Chutzpah Crown: 'Anti-Semitism Victim' Bernie Begs for Mercy," *New York Post*, June 24, 2009.

52. B. Golding and D. Mangan, "Madoff Mauled over 'Heir' Mail: Big Bucks Gifts a Bid to Stash Loot: Feds," *New York Post*, January 6, 2009.

53. Anti-Defamation League, "ADL Survey: Anti-Semitism in America Remains Constant; 15 Percent of Americans Hold 'Strong' Anti-Semitic Beliefs," last modified November 1, 2007, www.adl.org/PresRele/ASUS_12/5159_12.htm.

54. A. Foxman, "Blaming the Jews: The Financial Crisis and Anti-Semitism," remarks at Anti-Defamation League Annual Meeting, Los Angeles, November 13, 2008, www.adl.org/main_Anti_Semitism_International/Blaming_Jews_Financial.htm.

55. Anti-Defamation League, "Anti-Semitism and the Madoff Scandal," last modified December 19, 2008, www.adl.org/main_Anti_Semitism_Domestic/Anti-Semitism+and+the+Madoff+Scandal.htm.

56. N. Malhotra and Y. Margalit, "Anti-Semitism and the Economic Crisis," *Boston Review* (May/June 2009), http://bostonreview.net/archives/BR34.3/malhotra_margalit.php.

57. B. Burston, "The Madoff Betrayal: Life Imitates Anti-Semitism," *Haaretz*, December 8, 2008, www.haaretz.com/jewish/2.209/bradley-burston-the-madoff-betrayal-life-imitates-anti-semitism-1.259625.

Chapter 3

1. "The Future of the Stockmarket," roundtable with Justin Fox, Ailsa Roell, Robert A. Schwartz, Muriel Seibert, and Josh Stampfli, October 20, 2007. Philoctetes Center, NY.

2. T. Francis, "SEC's Cox Catches Blame for Financial Crisis," Bloomberg.com, September 19, 2008, www.bloomberg.com/news/articles/2008-09-19/secs-cox-catches-blame-for-financial-crisisbusinessweek-business-news-stock-market-and-financial-advice.

3. J. Westbrooke and R. Schmidt, "Cox 'Asleep at the Switch' as Paulson, Bernake Encroach," Bloomberg.com, September 21, 2008, www.bloomberg.com/news/articles/2008-09-22/cox-asleep-at-switch-as-paulson-bernanke-encroach-ikhm3wqz.

4. R. Smith, "Wall Street Mystery Features a Big Board Rival," *Wall Street Journal*, December 16, 1992.

5. "Investigation of Failure of the SEC to Uncover Bernard Madoff's Ponzi Scheme (Public Version)," Securities and Exchange Commission, www.sec.gov/news/studies/2009/oig-509.pdf.

6. K. Scannell, "Madoff Chasers Dug for Years, to No Avail," *Wall Street Journal*, January 5, 2009.

7. S. Will, "America's Ponzi Culture," in Will, Handelman, and Brotherton, *How They Got Away With It*.

8. P. Krugman, "The Madoff Economy," *New York Times*, December 19, 2008.

9. D. Retter and A. Geller, "How the SEC Bozos Blew It," *New York Post*, February 5, 2009.

10. "The SEC We Deserve," *Washington Post*, November 3, 2009.

11. "You Mean That Bernie Madoff?" *New York Times*, December 19, 2009.

12. Z. Kouwe, "Those Who Lost Savings Find Little Comfort," *New York Times*, March 11, 2009.

13. From December 16, 2008.

14. L. McShane, "Madoff Made Mockery of Feckless SEC," *Daily News* (NY), February 9, 2009.

15. S. Labaton, "SEC Image Suffers in a String of Setbacks," *New York Times*, December 15, 2008.

16. C. Seib, "SEC Failings Laid Bare as Madoff Tape Comes to Light," *Times* (London), September 11, 2009.

17. Z. A. Goldfarb, "The Madoff Files: A Chronicle of SEC Failure; Over and Over, Agency Skipped 'Basic' Steps to Find Fraud, Report Says," *Washington Post*, September 3, 2009.

18. M. Goldstein, "Madoff Accountant Avoids Prison Term," *New York Times*, May 28, 2015.

19. Securities Investor Protection Corporation. See their website, www.sipc.org.

20. A. Clark, "Financial: Judge Is Urged to Jail Madoff for $1M Giveaway to Friends and Family: Prosecutor Says Financier Sidestepped Asset Freeze: Watchdogs Are Urged to Quit over Scrutiny Failures," *Guardian*, January 6, 2009.

21. P. Tharp, "SEC's Porn Again—Staff Spent Hours Surfing Sexxxy Sites at Work," *New York Post*, February 5, 2009.

22. The Keystone Cops were famous during the era of silent movies. They were noted for their slapstick antics, lengthy wild-goose chases, and general inability to accomplish any productive police work. *Columbo* centered on the adventures and work of Lieutenant Frank Columbo, played by actor Peter Falk. In a sense, the reference to Columbo as a bureaucratic bumbler is misguided; the SEC would have been lucky to have Columbo aboard. Although he appeared as incompetent, at the end of each episode Columbo had apprehended the crook of the week.

23. S. Jagger, "SEC Ignored My Warnings, Says Madoff Whistleblower," *Times* (London), February 5, 2009.

24. McShane, "Madoff Made Mockery."

25. L. Mongelli and D. Mangan, from February 5, 2009.

26. M. Lewis and D. Einhorn, "The End of the Financial World as We Know It," *New York Times*, January 4, 2009.

27. The SEC in 2013 put forth new rules explicitly intended to prevent another Madoff-like incident from occurring.

28. J. Sterngold, "Unraveling the Lies That Madoff Told," *Wall Street Journal*, December 10, 2013.

29. Fifteen people have pled guilty or been convicted in connection to the scam, although "prosecutors conceded Madoff alone knew the full extent of his deception." Included in this list is Bernie Madoff's brother, Peter Madoff, who was sentenced to ten years. See J. Ax, "With Final Defendant, Madoff Case Comes to an End," Reuters, August 4, 2015.

30. D. Callahan, *The Cheating Culture* (Orlando: Harcourt, 2004), 246.

31. J. B. Steward: "Bernard L. Madoff was no evil genius. He was a pretty bad liar at every step of the way—and the investigators knew it."

32. B. Appelbaum and D. S. Hilzenrath, "SEC Didn't Act on Madoff Tips," *Washington Post*, December 16, 2008.

33. P. Tharp and M. DeCambre, "Wall Street's Cops Beat—Cox and Levitt Trade Barbs over Fighting Frauds," *New York Post*, December 18, 2008.

34. "You Mean That Bernie Madoff?"

35. A. R. Paley and D. S. Hilzenrath, "SEC Chief Defends His Restraint; Cox Rebuffs Criticism of Leadership during Crisis," *Washington Post*, December 24, 2008.

36. R. M. Merelman, *Partial Visions: Culture and Politics in Britain, Canada, and the United States* (Madison: University of Wisconsin Press, 1991).

37. A. Clark, "Obama Promises 'Adult Supervision' for Wall Street: Recent Scandals Blamed on Free-market Dogma," *Guardian*, December 19, 2008.

38. A. Clark, "National: Madoff Scandal: Regulation: Light Touch, Laissez Faire, or Simply Anything Goes?" *Guardian*, December 16, 2008.

39. A. Clark, "The Bush Years: The Economy," *Guardian*, January 17, 2009.

40. S. de Bruxelles, "Ex-soldier Shot Himself after Losing Savings in Madoff Scams," *Times* (London), January 12, 2009.

41. A. Clark, "Madoff Scandal: Global Trail of Victims of the Man of the 17th Floor: RBS and HSBC among Major Banks to Admit Losses from $50bn Wall Street Fraud," *Guardian*, December 19, 2008.

42. "Financial: Viewpoint Madoff, the Midas Who Made an Ass of Investors," *Guardian*, December 16, 2008.

43. C. Ayres, "At Last! Someone We Can Blame for Our Woes," *Times* (London), December 20, 2008.

44. P. Inman, "National: Madoff Scandal: Pyramids of Deceit: How Ponzi Schemes Work," *Guardian*, December 16, 2008.

45. Ibid.

46. "Bust Bankers" (editorial), *Sun*, December 16, 2008.

47. "Boards and Rewards," *Times* (London), February 23, 2008.

48. W. Rees-Mogg, "We Will Sink, Not Swim, in a Sea of New Rules; Pay Controls Are a Sign of Panic; Leaders from Edward III to Edward Heath Have Discovered That They Do Not Work," *Times* (London), September 7, 2008.

49. "You Mean That Bernie Madoff?"

50. "Keystone Kop of Wall St," *New York Post*, December 13, 2008.

51. S. Mallaby, "End of the Hedge Fund" (editorial), *Washington Post*, December 13, 2008, A25.

52. T. Murakami Tse, "For Hedge Funds, Biggest Fear Is More Regulation," *Washington Post*, June 25, 2009.

53. R. J. Samuelson, "American Capitalism Besieged," *Washington Post*, March 23, 2009.

54. "Boards and Rewards," *Times* (London), February 23, 2008.

55. Ibid.

56. N. Hertz, "Goodbye Gucci," *Times* (London), February 25, 2009.

57. D. Roberts, "Comment and Debate: Debt Has Become a Drug. Withdrawal Will Be Painful," *Guardian*, January 30, 2009.

58. See R. DeVos, *Compassionate Capitalism: People Helping People Help Themselves* (New York: Plume, 1994).

Chapter 4

1. P. Arestis and E. Karakitsos, "Financial Market Puzzles May Affect World Growth," *Challenge* 48 (2005): 95–113.

2. G. Irvin, "Inequality and Recession in Britain: Findings from Economic and Social Research," Economic and Social Research Council, 2009, www.swslim.org.uk/downloads/recession/publications/recession_britain.pdf.

3. T. Warren, *Fragile Middle Class: Americans in Debt* (New Haven, CT: Yale University Press, 2000).

4. P. K. Brooks, "Households Hit Hard by Wealth Losses," International Monetary Fund, June 24, 2009, www.imf.org/external/pubs.ft/survey/so/2009/num06409a.htm.

5. P. Gregg and J. Wadsworth, "The UK Labour Market and the 2008–2009 Recession," Centre for Economic Performance, London School of Economics, 2010, http://eprints.lse.ac.uk/28758/1/op025.pdf.

6. Ibid.

7. R. Vaitilingam, "Recession Britain: Findings from Economic and Social Research," Economic and Social Research Council, 2009, http://swslim.org.uk/downloads/recession/publications/recession_britain.pdf.

8. G. Irvin, "Inequality and Recession in Britain and the USA," *Development and Change* 42 (2011): 154–82.

9. *New York Post*, December 16, 2008.

10. T. Zambito, "Ponzi King Eyes One Last Move—Pleas Deal Pros Point to Legal Wrangling, Vics Would Get Their Say," *Daily News* (NY), March 7, 2009.

11. E. Hays, "Add Rev. Al to Madoff's Enemy List," *Daily News* (NY), February 8, 2009.

12. C. Haberman, "Is 150 Appropriate, or Just Silly?" *New York Times*, July 3, 2009.

13. See, for example, B. Weiser, "Madoff Judge Recalls Rationale for Imposing 150-year Sentence," *New York Times*, June 29, 2011. See also T. Zambito, "Bernie Pleads for Break, Says He's Sorry and 71," *Daily News* (NY), June 24, 2009.

14. T. Zambito and C. Siemaszko, "He's Entering Court and May Never See Outside Again," *Daily News* (NY), March 12, 2009.

15. K. B. Richburg and T. Murakami Tse, "Despite Madoff Guilty Plea, Questions Swirl and Rage Boils; Victims Gather at Courthouse as Financier Reports to Jail," *Washington Post*, March 12, 2009.

16. A. Clark, "Madoff Affair: 'He Deserves No Better than to Live under a Bridge in a Cardboard Box'; Victims of $65bn Fraud Vent Their Fury as Judge Ponders Sentence," *Guardian*, June 17, 2009.

17. Hays, "Add Rev. Al to Madoff's Enemy List."

18. D. Jones, "King Con Stole Our Lives: British Widow Tells How She Fell Victim to Bernie Madoff," *Daily Mail*, January 16, 2009.

19. L. Browning, "The Loneliest Woman in New York," *New York Times*, June 12, 2009.

20. Ibid.

21. P. Huguenin and G. Salamone, "The Cursed Wives Club Shame and Blame Follow Scammers' Spouses," *Daily News* (NY), June 30, 2009.

22. A. Clark, "Financial: Wall Street Scandal: 'I Knew This Would Come'—Madoff Jailed as He Admits $65bn Fraud: Disgraced Financier Faces 150-year Sentence: Victims Complain That Fraudster Avoided Full Trial," *Guardian*, March 13, 2009.

23. J. Nocera, "Madoff Had Accomplices: His Victims," *New York Times*, March 14, 2009.

24. Z. Kouwe, "Waiting to See Madoff, an Angry Crowd Is Disappointed," *New York Times*, June 30, 2009.

25. P. Furman, T. Zambito, and D. Feiden, "We Blew It, SEC Admits; Turned Blind Eye to Warnings on Madoff," *Daily News*, December 17, 2008.

26. D. Henriques, "At Madoff Hearing, Lawmakers Lay Into SEC," *New York Times*, February 5, 2009.

27. T. Zambito and D. Feiden, "Madoff Is Accused of a New Con; Mailed $1M in Gems to Pals, Feds Say," *Daily News* (NY), January 6, 2009.

28. S. Ranulf, *Moral Indignation and Middle Class Psychology* (Levin & Munksgaard, 1938).

29. N. Hertz, "Goodbye Gucci: It's the Age of Co-op Capitalism; From the Wreckage of Recession a New Economic Order Is Emerging, Based on Collaboration and the Collective Interest," *Times* (London), February 25, 2009.

30. Thorstein Veblen, *Theory of the Leisure Class* (New York: Dover, 1994).

31. A. Stanley, "Scandals to Warm To," *New York Times*, December 21, 2008.

32. Browning, "Loneliest Woman."

33. D. Willetts, "Madoff Sell-Off," *Sun*, September 10, 2009.

34. D. Segal, "Recession Pain, Even in Palm Beach," *New York Times*, April 11, 2009.

35. S. Jagger, C. Seib, and P. Hosking, "British Banks Losing Billions to 'One Big Lie,' in Biggest Ever Fraud; Wall Street Investors Struggle to Understand How They Fell for Simple Pyramid-selling Fraud," *Times* (London), December 16, 2008.

36. In the bankruptcy proceedings, the attorneys for Irving H. Picard, trustee for the SIPA liquidation of Bernard L. Madoff Investment Securities LLC, documented extensively the instances in which Madoff's fraudulent investment advisory business (and

hence investor funds) was used to finance either personal expenditures or prop up other Madoff business demands. For example, BLMIS funds were used to purchase properties for his sons, ownership shares in a private jet, yachts, and for contributions to Madoff Energy, which was owned by his sons and niece. "There are many more examples demonstrating Madoff's complete disregard for any corporate formality," attorneys David Sheehan and Marc Hirschfield would note.

37. T. Zambito and C. Siemaszko, "Well, Loot What's in His Goodie Bag! Madoff Had Boats and Homes and Jewels and Cash—$826M Total," *Daily News* (NY), March 14, 2009.

38. "G2: Organised Crime: Finance," *Guardian*, September 9, 2009.

39. B. Golding, "The Ruth Hurts—Madoff Wife on Subway—With 99 Cents Ad," *New York Post*, June 25, 2009.

40. C. Bray, "Madoff Lists $826 Million in Assets, Give or Take," *Wall Street Journal*, March 14, 2009.

41. Golding, "The Ruth Hurts."

42. Browning, "Loneliest Woman."

43. S. Cahalan, "Bernie Madoff's Wife Seeking Redemption through Charity Work in Florida," *New York Post*, July 18, 2010.

44. "From High Life to Household Chores," *Daily Mail*, March 14, 2012; and D. Mangan and L. Babcock, "Ruth's Trashy New Life," *New York Post*, March 14, 2012.

45. A. Clark, "Financial: Madoff Spends Jail Time with a Brooklyn Mobster and a Spy for Israel, Lawsuit Reveals," *Guardian*, October 22, 2009.

46. B. Golding, D. Montero, and L. I. Alpert, "Jailbird Bernie Already Crying—Begs Release and Loneliness of 'The Box,'" *New York Post*, March 14, 2009.

47. T. Zambito, "It's Penthouse to the Federal Pen for Bernie; From Park Ave. Splendor to a Prison Cell," *Daily News* (NY), June 30, 2009.

48. "Madoff's People: The Architect of History's Biggest Fraud Depended on So Many Others to Perpetrate His Crime That His Downfall Must Be Seen as an Indictment of His Era," *Times* (London), December 23, 2008.

49. M. Lupica, "Unbridled Greed Chips Away at Last Remnants of the American Dream," *Daily News* (NY), December 15, 2008.

50. "Voice of Daily Mirror: 'Off to Prison,'" *Daily Mirror*, March 13, 2009.

51. M. Austin, "Wellworth's Wonder Woman," *Daily Mirror*, March 15, 2009.

52. S. Hawkes, "myView," *Sun*, December 16, 2008.

53. A. Applebaum, "What a Member of Parliament Deserves" (editorial), *Washington Post,* May 26, 2009.

54. A political meme circulating on social media as late as September 2015 almost heroically proclaimed of Madoff, "Why is Bernie Madoff the only Wall St. Criminal to face jail time? Because he robbed the 1%, not the 99%."

55. Even academics would express support for such a narrative. In H. van de Bunt, "Walls of Secrecy and Silence: The Madoff Case and Cartels in the Construction Industry," *Criminology and Public Policy* 9 (2010), he writes, "In hindsight, we can conclude that Madoff's concealment was far from perfect and that at least a large part of the 'mys-

tery' surrounding the longevity of his fraud lies in the uncritical attitude adopted by thousands of his victims." He does not distinguish between different types of investors and their varying levels of financial literacy and awareness.

56. F. Norris, "The Money Is Gone: Now What?" *New York Times*, March 20, 2009.

57. P. Sullivan, "The Rules That Madoff's Investors Ignored," *New York Times*, January 6, 2009.

58. E. Robinson, "The Year of Madoff," *Washington Post*, December 30, 2008.

59. G. Younge, "Greed Has Pushed Political Credibility and Financial Trust into Freefall: Recent Scandals in America Reveal a Value System That Puts the Wealth of a Few Before the Welfare of Many," *Guardian*, December 22, 2008.

60. C. Mortished, "Scandal Blows a Hole in the Credibility of Investment Managers," *Times* (London), December 17, 2008.

61. H. Karoliszyn, K. Porpora, and S. Goldsmith, "Vics Declare Outcome a Bittersweet Victory; We Gave Him Trust, Money and Lost Everything," *Daily News* (NY), June 30, 2009.

62. "Rotter in Jail," *Daily Mirror*, June 30, 2009.

63. T. Zambito, "Bernie's Vics Are Mad(off) as Hell in Letters to Judge," *Daily News* (NY), June 16, 2009.

64. T. Zambito, "Ponzi King's Day of Reckoning Finally Arrives," *Daily News* (NY), June 29, 2009.

65. J. Fermino, "Congress Probes How SEC Blew It," *New York Post*, January 6, 2009.

66. J. Bone, "'Evil' Madoff Gets 150 Years; Victims Applaud as $65bn Fraudster Is Sentenced," *Times* (London), June 30, 2009.

67. A. Clark, "Financial: Wall Street Scandal: 'Worse than the Mafia': Victims Don't Get Their Day in Court," *Guardian*, March 13, 2009.

68. Clark, "Madoff Affair: 'He Deserves no Better than to Live Under a Bridge in a Cardboard Box.'"

69. J. Schwartz, "Lost in Bernie's Shadow," *New York Times*, April 12, 2009.

70. J. Nocera, "Madoff Had Accomplices: His Victims," *New York Times*, March 13, 2009, sec. B.

71. K. McCoy, "Madoff Victims Describe Pain of Fraud to Judge," *USA Today*, June 16, 2009.

72. T. Dowling, "G2: This Weekend's TV: In Attempting to Explain His Epic Fraud, the Madoff Hustle Gave Us More Insults than Facts," *Guardian*, June 29, 2009.

73. Henriques, *Wizard of Lies*.

74. "Madoff Victim Fund: May 2015 Update," Department of Justice Asset Forfeiture Distribution Program, http://madoffvictimfund.com/May2015_Update.shtml.

75. Madoff Victim Fund, http://madoffvictimfund.com/.

76. J. Bernstein, "Madoff Client Jeffrey Picower Netted $5 Billion—More than Madoff Himself," *ProPublica*, June 23, 2009. Picower was found dead in a pool after allegedly suffering a heart attack in 2009. He was sued by the bankruptcy trustee, Irving Picard, for $7.2 billion and his wife agreed to the forfeiture, although she insisted her husband in no way knew about the fraud.

77. FBI Press Release, December 7, 2010, www.fbi.gov/newyork/press-releases/2010/nyfo120710.htm. Shapiro's family agreed to forfeit $625 million to the government without admission of wrongdoing.

78. State of California Department of Justice Press Release, September 22, 2009. https://oag.ca.gov/news/press-releases/brown-sues-beverly-hills-investment-adviser-stanley-chais-misleading-investors.

79. SIPA trustee Irving Picard used "clawback" litigation to attempt to recover assets from "net winners" to distribute among "net losers." In dozens of these lawsuits, he argued that they should have known about the fraud.

80. Bloomberg, "Trade-worker Funds Lose Appeal to Recover Madoff Losses," *Pensions and Investments*, February 22, 2013, www.pionline.com/article/20130222/ONLINE/130229938/trade-worker-funds-lose-appeal-to-recover-madoff-losses.

81. The term "superpredator" was coined by Princeton professor John DiIulio to denote young offenders who were animalistic in their violent impulses, wreaking mayhem in their communities.

82. M. Jacobson, *Downsizing Prisons: How to Reduce Crime and End Mass Incarceration* (New York: NYU Press, 2005).

83. S. Cohen, *Folk Devils and Moral Panics* (New York: Routledge, 2002).

84. S. Crouch, "Whether the Weapon Is a Pencil or Hot Lead, a Thug's Still a Thug," *Daily News* (NY), July 6, 2009.

85. P. Flanagan, "Two-tier Justice System? You Can Bank on That," *Daily Mirror*, October 2, 2009; and M. Fitzmaurice, "Justice Turns a Blind Eye to Super Rich," *Daily Mirror*, February 18, 2009.

86. K. Macdonald, "Give Us Laws That The City Will Respect and Fear," *Times* (London), February 23, 2009.

87. L. Celona, K. Fasick, and D. Mangan, "Madoff: I'm Weakened at 'Bernie's'—Park Ave. 'Prisoner's' Fury," *New York Post*, January 29, 2009.

88. J. Molloy, "Take Comfort, Crooks: Judges May Send You to Posh Pad Instead of Jail," *Daily News* (NY), January 7, 2009.

89. M. Daly, "The City's Star Crook: Fed Entourage Protects Madoff," *Daily News* (NY), January 6, 2009.

90. C. Seib, "Madoff Waits in His Penthouse for a Court to Jail Him, Too," *Times* (London), January 12, 2009.

91. R. K. Merton, "Social Structure and Anomie," *American Sociological Review* 3 (1938): 672–82.

Chapter 5

1. J. Kemp, C. Boyle, B. Paddock, and L. McShane, "They Came to See Him Go," *Daily News*, March 13, 2009.

2. B. Golding, R. Fenton, and D. Mangan, "Madoff 'Family Plot,'" *New York Post*, March 11, 2009.

3. J. Molloy, "Take Comfort, Crooks: Judges May Send You to Posh Pad Instead of Jail like Madoff," *Daily News* (NY), January 7, 2009.

4. S. Strom, "Elie Wiesel Levels Scorn at Madoff," *New York Times*, February 26, 2009.

5. The counts facing Madoff were securities fraud, investment adviser fraud, mail fraud, wire fraud, international money laundering to promote specified unlawful activity, international money laundering to conceal and disguise the proceeds of specified unlawful activity, money laundering, false statements, perjury, making a false filing with the SEC, and theft from an employee benefit plan.

6. H. Garfinkel, "Conditions of Successful Degradation Ceremonies," *American Journal of Sociology* 61 (1956): 420–24.

7. R. Blecker, letter to the editor, *New York Times*, July 1, 2009.

8. V. Belenkaya and B. Hutchinson, "Live a Long Life in Hell, Vics Says," *Daily News* (NY), March 11, 2009.

9. J. Bone, "Madoff Will Heat Victims' Fury as He Is Sentenced; Conman Is Expected to Get at Least 20 Years in Jail," *Times* (London), June 29, 2009.

10. J. Marino and R. Schapiro, "Bernie Should Rot with the Rats, Vic's Pal Says," *Daily News* (NY), December 26, 2008.

11. R. Sandomir, "In the Matter of . . . Federal Judge Holds Financial Fate of Wilpon and Katz," *New York Times*, July 7, 2009.

12. B. Golding, J. MacIntosh, and D. Mangan, "Crash & Bernie after 'Evil' Con—DC Probe Eyed as Scandal Toll Rises," *New York Post*, December 16, 2008.

13. J. Molloy, "Bernie's Hand in Grave; Family of Beloved Rabbi Who Died in 2000 Has to Sell It All," *Daily News* (NY), March 8, 2009.

14. Belenkaya and Hutchinson, "Live a Long Life in Hell."

15. B. Golding, "Poison-Pen Letters: May He Bern in Hell!" *New York Post*, March 21, 2009.

16. K. Whitehouse, "Devil in the Details: 'Clawback' Suits Seek $54B for Madoff Victims," *New York Post*, December 10, 2010.

17. *Daily News* (NY), March 7, 2009.

18. See, for example, artist J. D. Crowe's "Pocket Watchdog Chris Cox SEC" from December 2008, www.cagle.com/jd-crowe/2008/12/pocket-watchdog-chris-cox-sec; the caricature that appeared in the Miami *Nuevo Herald* in 2008, http://fineartamerica.com/featured/bernard-madoff-caricatures-by-pontet.html; and Randy Bish's "Madoff 150 Years in Jail" for the *Pittsburgh Tribune-Review* in June 2009, www.cagle.com/randy-bish/2009/06/bernie-madoff-3.

19. "Bernie in Hell Hotsauce Launched," *Telegraph*, January 11, 2009.

20. "Mini Madoff Turns Heads at Toy Fair," *New York Times*, DealBook, February 17, 2009.

21. *The Devil and the Jews: The Medieval Conception of the Jew and Its Relation to Modern Anti-Semitism* (Philadelphia: Jewish Publication Society, 1984). Also see R. Rockaway and A. Gutfeld, "Demonic Images of the Jew in 19th century United States," *American Jewish History* 89 (2001): 355; S. Menache, "Faith, Myth, and Politics: The Stereotype of the Jews and Their Expulsion from England and France," *Jewish Quarterly Review* 4 (1985): 351–74; and A. Edwards, A. Wurm, and M. Castillo, "Lost in Translation:

Anti-Semitic Stereotypes Based on Mistranslation," *University of North Carolina at Chapel Hill Jewish Studies Program*, https://jewishstudies.unc.edu/files/2015/12/Edwards.Final_.pdf.

22. R. Pogrebin, "For Jews, Madoff Scandal Brings Feelings of Betrayal and Shame," *New York Times*, December 24, 2008.

23. "She's Either the Heroine Who Stood Up to Bernie Madoff—or the Worst Kind of Rich Bitch," *Times Magazine* (London), March 13, 2009.

24. R. Bluementhal, "Ideas & Trends: If Bernie Met Dante," *New York Times*, March 15, 2009.

25. T. Zambito, J. Martinez, and C. Siemaszko, "Madoff's Pine Box Sentence; With 150-year Term, Ponzi Con Man Will Die in Prison," *Daily News* (NY), June 30, 2009.

26. T. Harris, letter to the editor, *Sun*, July 3, 2009.

27. C. Moffat, letter to the editor, *Sun*, July 2, 2009.

28. K. MacKenzie, "Don't Shed Tears for Hacker Gary," *Sun*, August 6, 2009.

29. "Untouchable Bankers Still Living It Up" (editorial), *Daily Mirror*, October 16, 2010.

30. P. Flanagan, "Rotten Anglo Costs Us Life & Limb ... Or EUR20K a Minute," *Daily Mirror*, September 3, 2010.

31. "The Wages of Sin: Madoff's Life Sentence Should Galvanize Regulators Everywhere, Including Britain," *Times* (London), June 30, 2009.

32. See Garland, *Peculiar Institution* (Harvard University Press, 2010); and Zimring, *The Contradictions of American Capital Punishment* (Oxford University Press, 2004).

33. "EU Policy on the Death Penalty," European Union, http://eeas.europa.eu/human_rights/ adp/index_en.htm, accessed April 23, 2013.

34. A. Cowell, "European Response Focuses on the Death Penalty," *New York Times*, December 30, 2006.

35. "Less Support for Death Penalty, Especially among Democrats," Pew Research Center, April 16, 2015.

36. C. Appleton and B. Grover, "The Pros and Cons of Life without Parole," *British Journal of Criminology* 47 (2007): 597–615.

37. D. Henriques, "Madoff, Apologizing, Is Given 150 Years," *New York Times*, June 30, 2009.

38. "Bernie Beats the Rap" (editorial), *Daily News* (NY), March 13, 2009.

39. Southern District Reporters, P.C. United States of America v. Bernard L. Madoff, New York, NY. March 12, 2009. 09 CCR 213 (DC).

40. B. Weiser, "Madoff Judge Recalls Rationale for Imposing 150-year Sentence," *New York Times*, June 29, 2011.

41. "Madoff's People; The Architect of History's Biggest Fraud Depended on So Many Others to Perpetrate His Crimes That His Downfall Must Be Seen as an Indictment of His Era," *Times* (London), December 23, 2008.

42. "Rotter in Jail," *Daily Mirror*, June 30, 2009.

43. T. Zambito, J. Martinez, and C. Siemaszko, "Have Fun in Your Fetid Little Cell; In a Blink He Goes from Posh Penthouse to the Horrid Life of a Common Crook," *Daily News* (NY), March 13, 2009.

44. Z. Kouwe, "Madoff's Lawyers See 12-year Term, Citing His Shame," *New York Times*, June 24, 2009.

45. D. Henriques, "U.S. Proposes 150 Years for Madoff," *New York Times*, June 27, 2009.

46. Z. Kouwe, "Waiting to See Madoff, an Angry Crowd Is Disappointed," *New York Times*, June 30, 2009.

47. P. J. Henning, "Long Sentences Send a Message Few May Hear," *New York Times*, June 27, 2011, DealBook.

48. "Ponzi Database," Ponzi Tracker, www.ponzitracker.com/ponzi-database/.

49. M. A. Galvin, "Sentencing Corporate Crime: Responses to Scandal and Sarbanes-Oxley," master's thesis, University of Maryland, 2015.

50. Ponzi Tracker.

51. J. D. Unnever, M. L. Benson, and F. T. Cullen, "Public Support for Getting Tough on Corporate Crime: Racial and Political Divides," *Journal of Research in Crime and Delinquency* 45 (May 2008): 163–90.

52. J. S. Rakoff, "The Financial Crisis: Why Have No High-Level Executives Been Prosecuted?" *New York Times*, January 9, 2014.

53. *The Financial Crisis Inquiry Report: Final Report of the National Commission on the Causes of the Financial and Economic Crisis in the United States* (Washington, DC: Financial Crisis Inquiry Commission, 2011).

54. Charles Gasparino accused Madoff of lying to him about collaborating with a Harvard business professor on a course in his article, "Madoff: I'm a Victim Too," FoxBusiness.com, August 25, 2011, after which Madoff labeled him a "hatchet-man." Although Harvard denied having any involvement with Madoff for months, eventually the university did admit that one of its professors was doing independent research with Madoff. Madoff also temporarily cut off communication with Diana Henriques after her book placed the inception of the fraud at an earlier date than Madoff claims.

55. N. Raymond and N. Brown, "Madoff's Younger Brother Sentenced to 10 Years for Role in Fraud," *Chicago Tribune*, December 20, 2012.

56. T. Hays, "Peter Madoff Pleads Guilty, to Serve 10 Years for Megafraud," *USA Today*, June 29, 2012.

57. Securities and Exchange Commission, "SEC Charges Goldman Sachs with Fraud in Structuring and Marketing of CDO Tied to Subprime Mortgages," April 16, 2010, www.sec.gov/news/press/2010/2010-59.htm.

58. Will, "America's Ponzi Culture."

59. D. Indiviglio, "Why Was Goldman's 2010 Profit Down 38%?" *Atlantic*, January 19, 2011.

60. The *New York Times* has made available documents from the Senate Permanent Subcommittee on Investigations relating to its inquiry into the financial crisis in April 2010. Among these are exhibit e-mails from Goldman Sachs executives discussing mortgage-backed securities and CDOs, as well as statements from the subcommittee on the exhibits; http://documents.nytimes.com/goldman-sachs-internal-emails.

61. See D. Matza and G. Sykes, "Techniques of Neutralization: A Theory of Delinquency," *American Sociological Review* 22 (1957): 664–70. They write, "It is our argument

that much delinquency is based on what is essentially an unrecognized extension of defenses to crimes, in the form of justifications for deviance that are seen as valid by the delinquent but not by the legal system of society at large." Among these techniques are denial of responsibility, denial of injury, denial of the victim, condemnation of the condemners, and the appeal to higher loyalties.

62. *Ice Libor*, www.theice.com/iba/libor.

63. A. Monticini and D. L. Thornton, "The Effect of Underreporting on Libor Rates," *Federal Reserve Bank of St. Louis Research Division*, Working Paper 2013-008A, February 2013, https://research.stlouisfed.org/wp/2013/2013-008.pdf.

64. M. Corkery and B. Protess, "Rigging of Foreign Exchange Market Makes Felons of Top Banks," *New York Times*, May 20, 2015.

65. R. Winnett, "Libor Scandal May Have Cost Families Their Homes," *Telegraph*, July 2, 2012.

66. The Office of Foreign Assets Control, operating under the US Department of the Treasury, "administers and enforces economic and trade sanctions based on US foreign policy and national security goals against targeted foreign countries and regimes, terrorists, international narcotics traffickers, those engaged in activities related to the proliferation of weapons of mass destruction, and other threats to the national security, foreign policy or economy of the United States." See www.treasury.gov/resource-center/sanctions/Pages/default.aspx.

67. B. Protess and J. Silver-Greenberg, "HSBC to Pay $1.92 Billion to Settle Charges of Money Laundering," *New York Times*, December 10, 2012.

68. In August 2015 Tom Hayes, a former UBS and Citigroup trader, was sentenced to fourteen years in prison in connection with the rigging of LIBOR in the United Kingdom.

69. D. Garland, "Sociological Perspectives on Punishment," *Crime and Justice* 14 (1991): 115–65.

Chapter 6

Chapter title: Jean-Baptiste Alphonse Karr, from the French, "*Plus ça change, plus c'est la même chose.*"

1. D. Harvey, *The Enigma of Capital and the Crises of Capitalism* (Oxford: Oxford University Press, 2010).

2. The Occupy Movement did not begin ex nihilo in September 2011 simply because of some smart advertising. Earlier in the summer, in small gatherings on Beaver Street in Manhattan, a group of local organizers, international activists, and anarchists formed the New York City General Assembly, which planned the logistics and framing of the actions.

3. See D. Graeber, "Enacting the Impossible: Making Decisions by Consensus," in *This Changes Everything: Occupy Wall Street and the 99% Movement* (Positive Futures Network, 2011), 22–24.

4. A. Kroll, "How Occupy Wall Street Really Got Started," in *This Changes Everything*, 16–21.

5. M. Saba, "Wall Street Protestors Inspired by Arab Spring Movement," CNN, September 17, 2011, www.cnn.com/2011/09/16/tech/social-media/twitter-occupy-wall-street/.

6. R. Milkman, S. Luce, and P. Lewis, "Changing the Subject: A Bottom-Up Account of Occupy Wall Street in New York City," 2013; available from the City University of New York's Murphy Institute, https://media.sps.cuny.edu/filestore/1/5/7/1_a05051d211 7901d/1571_92f562221b8041e.pdf.

7. "Declaration of the Occupation of New York City," in *This Changes Everything*, 36–38.

8. S. Van Gelder, "How Occupy Wall Street Changes Everything," in *This Changes Everything*, 1–12.

9. "Bernie Sanders on the Issues," https://berniesanders.com/issues/.

10. "M20: Showdown at the Department of Justice," Occupy Wall Street, http://occupywallstreet.net/story/m20-showdown-department-justice.

11. C. Mead and S. Walker, "Anti-Wall Street Protestors Reach 'Prime Time' with Arrests," Bloomberg, October 2, 2011.

12. A. R. Sorkin, "On Wall Street, a Protest Matures," *New York Times,* October 3, 2011.

13. R. Quigley, "The Impulse Towards Individual Criminal Punishment after the Financial Crisis," *Virginia Journal of Social Policy and the Law* 22 (2014): 105–58.

14. Ibid., 108.

15. "United States Attorneys' Annual Statistics Report," 2012.

16. R. Mitchell, "Business; White-collar Criminal? Pack Lightly for Prison," *New York Times*, August 11, 2002.

17. "A Living Death: Life without Parole for Nonviolent Offenses," ACLU, November 2013, www.aclu.org/files/assets/111813-lwop-complete-report.pdf#page=23. These two offenses were fraud and money laundering.

18. A. Alvesalo and S. Tombs, "Working for Criminalization of Economic Offending: Contradictions for Critical Criminology?" *Critical Criminology* 11 (2002): 21–40.

19. D. Weisburd, E. Waring, and E. Chayet, "Specific Deterrence in a Sample of White-collar Crimes," *Criminology* 33 (1995): 587–607.

20. Levi, "Social Reactions to White-collar Crimes."

21. P. Gottschalk, "White Collar Crime and Police Crime: Rotten Apples or Rotten Barrels?" *Critical Criminology* 20 (2012): 169–82.

22. J. D. Unnever, M. L. Benson, and F. T. Cullen, "Public Support for Getting Tough on Corporate Crime: Racial and Political Divides," *Journal of Research in Crime and Delinquency* 45 (May 2008): 163–90.

23. P. Mirowski, *Never Let a Serious Crisis Go to Waste* (New York: Verso Books, 2013).

24. R. Wilson, "States Slow to Spend Billions in TARP Funds for Underwater Homeowners," *Washington Post*, October 30, 2013.

25. Barofsky, *Bailout*.

26. T. Greenstein, "The Fed's $16 Trillion Bailouts Under-Reported," *Forbes*, September 20, 2011.

27. See A. E. Wilmarth Jr., "The Dodd-Frank Act: A Flawed and Inadequate Response to the Too-Big-to-Fail Problem," *Oregon Law Review* 39 (2011): 951–1057. He

concludes: "Dodd-Frank's provisions fall short of the changes that would be needed to prevent future taxpayer-financed bailouts . . . [It] fails to make fundamental structural reforms that could largely eliminate the subsidies currently exploited by large complex financial institutions."

28. J. C. Coffee Jr. discusses what he aptly terms the "regulatory sine curve," wherein after economic crisis and a push to regulate, over time a "collective social amnesia" takes over and allows for deregulatory forces backed by superior resources and organization to again assume primacy. He pessimistically argues, "The Dodd-Frank Act's reforms will be marginalized over time." See his "Political Economy of Dodd-Frank: Why Financial Reform Tends to Be Frustrated and Systemic Risk Perpetuated," *Cornell Law Review* 97 (July 2012): 1019–82.

29. L. Abramowicz, "Goldman Sachs Hawks CDOs Tainted by Credit Crisis under New Name," Bloomberg, February 4, 2015.

30. G. Grey, "A Soulless Market: NYT Financial Analyst Diana Henriques Visits UT, Speaks on Financial Trust and the Mechanics behind Madoff's Epic Scheme," *Culture-Map Austin*, November 13, 2011.

31. See the complete platform at www.gop.com/the-2016-republican-party-plat-form/, accessed August 1, 2016.

32. "Trump to Propose Moratorium on New Financial Regulations," Bloomberg Politics, www.bloomberg.com/politics/articles/2016-08-08/trump-to-propose-moratorium -on-new-financial-regulations.

33. Fligstein and Roehrkasse, "Causes of Fraud in Financial Crises."

34. N. Ryder, "'Greed, for Lack of a Better Word, Is Good. Greed Is Right. Greed Works': A Contemporary and Comparative Review of the Relationship between the Global Financial Crisis, Financial Crime and White Collar Criminals in the U.S. and the U.K.," *British Journal of White Collar Crime* 1 (2016): 3–47. See also Fligstein and Roehrkasse, "Causes of Fraud in Financial Crises."

35. H. Pontell, "White Collar Crime or Just Risky Business? The Role of Fraud in Major Financial Debacles," *Crime, Law and Social Change* 42 (2004): 309–24.

36. In *The Cheating Culture*, David Callahan makes a similar argument, namely that the "money culture" that fully engulfed US society in the neoliberal period has transformed the cultural ethos for everyone, with serious moral ramifications. As aggressive monetary goals assume primacy over all other areas of life, the number of those who consider the "good life" as necessitating a "lot of money" has increased substantially. This push to achieve—and at any cost—creates an environment where cheating is assumed, rationalized, and normalized. "The yawning gap between winners and losers is . . . having a lethal effect on personal integrity," he claims. "In a society where winners win bigger than ever before and losers are punished more harshly . . . more and more people will do *anything* to be a winner . . . Cheating . . . is more tempting if the rewards for success are greater" (69). He cites a 2001 poll which found that almost half of all Americans indicated they had cheated, would cheat, or thought it was okay to cheat (177). Callahan's arguments are broadly analogous to those of sociologists Steven Messner and Richard Rosenfeld in their seminal *Crime and the American Dream*, 5th ed. (Boston: Cengage, 2012). Here Messner and Rosenfeld give us "institutional anomie"

theory, which argues that instrumental crimes (white-collar *and* street crime) are fueled by an American individualistic and materialistic cultural ideal that privileges the never-ending pursuit of wealth above all other social institutions, in spite of unequal structural opportunities. While their theory is difficult to test objectively and it doesn't fully account for individuals who do *not* engage in fraud, some empirical support, as it applies to white-collar crime offenders and victims, has been identified.

37. J. Young, "Bernie Madoff, Finance Capital, and Anomic Society," in *How They Got Away With It* (New York: Columbia University Press, 2013).

38. Levi, "Social Reactions to White-collar Crimes."

39. J. Ferrell, "Cultural Criminology," *Annual Review of Sociology* 25 (1999): 395–418.

40. T. Teachout, "Shame on Elie Wiesel," *Wall Street Journal,* August 13, 2010.

41. J. Brown, "'Imagining Madoff' Gives the Face of Evil a Voice," *Boston Globe,* January 4, 2014.

42. The Germanwings Flight 9525 case involved a copilot who deliberately crashed the plane into the French Alps, killing all 150 people on board, and led to an extensive investigation of his mental health prior to the incident.

43. As discussed in her book *Eichmann in Jerusalem: A Report on the Banality of Evil* (New York: Penguin Books, 1992).

44. K. Tierney, *Social Roots of Risk: Producing Disasters, Promoting Resilience* (Stanford, CA: Stanford University Press, 2014), 3–4. Noted sociologists such as Anthony Giddens and Ulrich Beck have taken an interest in theorizing risk and the "risk society." However, their conceptions of risk are not focused specifically on the consequences—social, psychological, and even biological—that have occurred in the past thirty or more years under finance-led capitalism, specifically financial liberalization, which has dismantled regulatory control over institutions, individuals, and products in the financial sector.

45. A. Ackerman, "Regulators Sound Alarm on High-frequency Trading Firms," *Wall Street Journal*, April 30, 2015.

46. See his *The Hour between Dog and Wolf: Risk-taking, Gut Feelings, and the Biology of Boom and Bust* (New York: Penguin, 2012). See also J. M. Coates and J. Herbert, "Endogenous Steroids and Financial Risk Taking on a London Trading Floor," *PNAS* 105 (2008): 6167–72.

47. J. E. Grable and So-Hyun Joo, "Environmental and Biopsychosocial Factors Associated with Financial Risk Tolerance," *Financial Counselling and Planning* 15(1) (2004). See also A. Bernasek and S. Shwiff, "Gender, Risk, and Retirement," *Journal of Economic Issues* 35:2 (2001): 345–56.

48. B. J. Carducci and A. S. Wong, "Type A and Risk-taking in Money Matters," *Journal of Business and Psychology* 12:3 (1998). See also the authors' "Sensation Seeking and Financial Risk Taking in Everyday Money Matters," *Journal of Business and Psychology* 5:4 (1991).

49. J. Sung and S. Hanna, "Factors Related to Risk Tolerance," *Financial Counseling and Planning* 7 (1996). They show how "performance statistics reported by Fairfield Sentry [a Madoff feeder fund] lie well outside their theoretical bounds."

50. See C. Bernard and P. Boyle, "Mr. Madoff's Amazing Returns: An Analysis of Split Strike Conversion Strategy," *Journal of Derivatives* 17:1 (2009).

51. D. Weisburd et al., *Crimes of the Middle Classes: White Collar Offenders in the Federal Courts* (New Haven, CT, and London: Yale University Press, 1991), 224.

52. H. N. Pontell and G. Geis, "How to Effectively Get Crooks like Bernie Madoff in Dutch," *Criminology and Public Policy* 9:3 (2010): 475, focus on policy suggestions. They do not believe that educating and alerting the public would significantly contribute to a decline in behavior like Madoff's. Rather they recommend changes to the employment of outside accounting firms to eliminate conflict of interest, the chartering of corporate entities federally, and rewriting the law defining the rights of corporations under the constitution. "Our policy recommendation is that a wholly distinctive body of law should be established that indicates what is and is not proper to corporates and should not resort to analogies of living human beings to make that determination." N. Reichman also uses the Madoff case in "Getting Our Attention," *Criminology and Public Policy* 9:3 (2010): 483, to rather argue broadly for more "political will" to probe and learn from mistakes, and for more funding for investigations.

53. D. Huynh, "Preemption v. Punishment: A Comparative Study of White Collar Crime Prosecution in the United States and the United Kingdom," *Journal of International Business and Law* 9 (July 24, 2000): 105–36.

54. D. McGurrin et al., "White Collar Crime Representation in the Criminological Literature Revisited, 2001–2010," *Western Criminology Review* 14:2 (2013): 3–19.

55. G. Barak, "The Flickering Desires for White-collar Crime Studies in the Post-financial Crisis: Will They Ever Shine Brightly?" *Western Criminology Review* 14:2 (2013): 61–71.

56. G. Geis, "White Collar Crime: What Is It?" *Current Issues in Criminal Justice* 3 (1991): 7–24.

57. In L. Snider, "The Sociology of Corporate Crime: An Obituary," *Theoretical Criminology* 4:2 (2000): 169–206, she remarks: "Corporations do not want nosey sociologists investigating their business practices. Unlike traditional offenders, they have the power to resist such incursions." She points out the lack of large-scale survey data which I have described. Because there is no large-scale "official" data, she says an "aura" of objectivity is lost when researchers have to produce their own small-scale numbers. See also Croall, *Understanding White Collar Crime.*

58. McGurrin et al., "White Collar Crime Representation."

59. C. Barnett, "The Measurement of White-collar Crime Data Using UCR Data," US Department of Justice.

60. D. O. Friedrichs, *Trusted Criminals: White Collar Crime in Contemporary Society* (New York: Wadsworth, 1996).

61. Office for National Statistics, www.ons.gov.uk/peoplepopulationandcommunity/crimeandjustice/articles/overviewoffraudstatistics/yearendingmarch2016.

62. www.ons.gov.uk/peoplepopulationandcommunity/crimeandjustice/bulletins/crimeinenglandandwales/2015-01-22#fraud.

63. G. Barak, "Doing Newsmaking Criminology within the Academy," *Theoretical Criminology* 11:2 (May 2007): 191–207.

INDEX